Madame de Staël

Atlas & Co.
New York

Madame de Staël
The First
Modern Woman

Francine
du Plessix Gray

Atlas & Co. *Publishers*
15 West 26th Street, 2nd floor
New York, NY 10010
www.atlasandco.com

Distributed to the trade by W. W. Norton & Company

Printed in the United States

Interior design by Yoshiki Waterhouse
Typesetting by Sara E. Stemen

Atlas & Company books may be purchased for educational,
business, or sales promotional use. For information, please
write to info@atlasandco.com.

Library of Congress Cataloging-in-Publication Data
is available upon request.

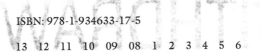

ISBN: 978-1-934633-17-5

13   12   11   10   09   08   1   2   3   4   5   6

To Jennifer

Contents

PART I

Happiness will come later; will come at intervals;
may never come.

    —Madame de Staël to her mother, January 1786

Chapter 1

Growing Up

It is the mid-1770s in a handsome house of the Parisian suburbs. The little girl and her father chase each other around the dining room table that stands by a window with a view of a lush green park, throwing napkins at each other's heads, laughing with unleashed merriment. The girl, Germaine, is tall for her age and sturdily built, with a full head of dark curly hair and swift, inquisitive, very beautiful hazel eyes. Her father, Jacques Necker, France's director of finance, is the nation's most powerful man after King Louis XVI. A small, trim man with a prim manner, he never allows himself this kind of romping except with his cherished only child. He stops briefly to wind a napkin around his head, turban-fashion, and then the two resume their chase, their shouts of laughter, until they hear the sound of familiar footsteps. It is the rigid Mme Necker, who does not tolerate such behavior at meals; who, in fact, would severely reprimand it upon any occasion. By the time Mme Necker enters the dining room father and daughter have stopped their games and are back in their seats, having resumed their breakfast in solemn silence.[1]

For Mme Suzanne Necker, née Curchod, lacks the vivacity of her daughter, and even of her habitually grave husband. Descended, like M. Necker, from a long line of Swiss Lutheran pastors, she is a former governess, and as the saying goes in Paris society, "When God created Mme Necker, He dipped her first into a bucket of starch."[2] Handsome and highly educated, but pedantic and a tad arrogant, she had been orphaned young and left penniless, and her romantic life, before she met M. Necker, had been limited to an ardent romance with the British historian Edward Gibbon, decades before he became fat and famous. Gibbon *père* had strenuously objected to the notion that his son might marry an impoverished foreigner, and Gibbon *fils,* to Mlle Necker's despair, called off their engagement. Still unmarried at the age of twenty-seven, Suzanne Curchod had resigned herself to the possibility of remaining a maiden lady. But that very year, while minding the children of a Parisian noblewoman, she had met a shy, unostentatious Swiss millionaire called Jacques Necker who proposed to her upon one of their first tête-à-têtes. And the boundless gratitude she owed her husband for having saved her from spinsterhood may well have contributed to the limitless devotion she offered him for the rest of her life.

As for M. Necker, his rise to power was due to the Catholic Church's ban on usury, which deterred France from ever having a banking system of its own: it had always relied on the Paris branches of Protestant banking houses, among which the Genevans were the most famous. Necker had made his first millions selling French and English treasury bonds, transactions made possible, after 1763, by the end of the Seven Years' War. Until the late 1760s this unostentatious mogul, who lived and dressed modestly, kept no mistress, and attended no important salons, was little known outside of Paris's banking circles. After a brilliant performance as head of the East India Company, Necker rose to prominence in the early years of Louis XVI's reign—the mid-1770s—when the king made him the head of the country's financial administration, with the title of Director General of Finance (since Necker was a foreigner he could not have a full ministerial post). Louis had at last come to realize that France was in an unprecedented state of penury. The modest, bluntly spoken financier was equally admired by the finicky Marie-Antoinette; he held the king's ear even more readily than the monarch's ministers, who grew increasingly resentful of Necker's influence.

It is possible that the enormous power Louis XVI offered Necker when he was still in his forties—a power made all the more unusual by the fact that he was a foreigner, a bourgeois, and a Protestant—may have heightened the financier's innate vanity. For although he was kind and trustworthy, and loyal to his democratic ideals, vanity was very much at the center of his character. The following portrait of him, penned by his wife shortly after their marriage, was not totally written in jest:

"Picture to yourself the most humorless fellow in the whole world . . . completely persuaded of his own superiority . . . so certain that he possesses every talent in the highest degree of perfection that he does not look elsewhere for instruction; never astonished by the littleness of others, because he is always enveloped in his own greatness . . . confounding men of substance with ignorant ones because he thinks they are all inferior to himself . . . preferring fools also because they make a more striking contrast with his own sublime genius."[3]

Mme Necker's sketch of her husband accords well with the bust Houdon made of Necker at the height of the financier's career: the haughtily tilted head, the complacently ironic smile, the half-closed eyes whose gaze seems absorbed in some profound insight. The financier's vanity must have been based on a high esteem of his own intelligence rather than of his looks: his large, stubborn, jutting chin, a forehead receding at an almost grotesque forty-five-degree angle, were topped by a pyramidal hairdo that became his comic trademark. Moreover Necker's conversation, which consisted, at best, of a profound and disdainful silence, was wretchedly ill-suited to Paris's wit-obsessed salons. Whatever these social flaws, his vanity offered him an Olympian calm that deepened the serenity of his marriage to the high-strung, hyperanxious Suzanne. She was obsessed with a fear of death, and in her thirties had already dictated, in her will, the bizarre manner in which she wanted to be buried: she wished to be placed in a glass coffin filled with formaldehyde, for her body to never decompose. This obsession with the funereal did not make her one pregnancy any easier. When her daughter Germaine was born, in 1766, she told all her friends that she had "suffered the tortures of the damned" during childbirth, that "death was ever at my bedside."[4] Being, like all French ladies of fashion, an ardent fan of Rousseau, she tried to breast-feed her child, but that too was a disaster. After "withstanding all the pains and tortures of that condition"[5] for a few months, she gave the baby to a big Flemish wet nurse just in time for Germaine not to die of starvation.

The child grew to be physically sturdy. But she barely survived the academic regimen her mother imposed on her, with a diligence that bordered on fanaticism, from the time she was a toddler. Highly ambitious for her daughter, and sensing the child's precocity, Suzanne force-fed her math, geography, science, languages, and theology from the time she was three. To teach her declamation, dance, and acting she hired the famous actress Mme Clairon (who, ironically, would later become a particularly bothersome mistress of Germaine's future husband). But Clairon was an exception. The power-hungry Suzanne refused to abandon to a stranger the education of a daughter she wished to be perfect. At the age of seven Germaine had not yet learned to run but danced perfectly. Aged twelve she was still forbidden to leave her house without her mother and was never allowed to play with other children but was already a walking encyclopedia of philosophical knowledge. Suzanne Necker worked under the delusion that she was bringing up Germaine according to the teachings of her idol, Rousseau, emulating the education offered to the hero of his novel *Émile*. But the differences were vast. Rousseau's Émile had barely learned his alphabet at an age when Germaine had read through her parents' entire library. Émile's tutor reserved the notion of God for the end of his pupil's education; Germaine, whose parents were devout Calvinists, knew her catechism before she was three. Émile was brought up in the country, safeguarded from the corrupting influences of society, whereas Germaine's education would be perfected in her mother's Paris drawing room, at the spacious house reserved on the rue de Cléry for the King's director of finance. And that was the one way in which Mme Necker gave her daughter an enormous advantage over other children: she immersed her in one of the last great salons of the ancien régime.

For notwithstanding her stiffness and her lack of spontaneity, in an effort to advance the fortunes of her cherished husband Mme Necker succeeded in creating the most brilliant Parisian salon of the 1770s and '80s. It was uphill all the way for her, through sheer discipline and perseverance. For the art of conversation—the meat and bones of any salon—was rooted in traditions set in the previous century by far more brilliant women, such great seventeenth-century *salonnières* as Mme de Rambouillet and the Marquise de Sablé. Rebelling against the swashbuckling crudeness of their male peers, who had been rendered particularly uncouth by decades of warfare, that generation of women had set out to recivilize France by purifying its language and its manners. And they created certain protocols of civilized conversation that would govern the art of discourse until the end of the ancien régime. Principal among such etiquettes was the notion of complaisance, a certain pliancy and malleability of mind that brought out the qualities of one's interlocutors, making them aware of talents they'd never known themselves to have. This could only be accomplished by a flexible, insinuating mind whose exertions must go unnoticed. "The government of a conversation," as Mme Necker herself would put it, "closely resembles that of a state: one must be barely aware of the authority that governs it."[6] Civil conversation, in fact, was seen as a means of attenuating malice and aggression and of moderating personal desire, thus becoming a form of spiritual exercise.

And yet the esprit at the heart of salon conversation also had to have a flirtatious, gossamer quality. Such naturalness and lightness of touch had become second nature for most women of the Parisian elite. But for a prim, provincial Swiss governess like Mme Necker, phenomenal concentration and diligence were required to learn the rules of the game. The earnest Suzanne had not an ounce of what Italians call *sprezzatura*—the appearance of engaging in any task with total ease and effortlessness—and was often candid about her anxiety. She was naive enough to say to one of her guests, "*Que voulez-vous, Madame,* one is not witty at will. . . . Look at M. Necker and see if he is amusing every day."[7] Necker was indeed absolutely hopeless in salon conversation and broke his silence only to make dull witticisms about men of letters with whom he believed his wife to be unduly taken. But such was his prestige that his muteness, and his restless entrances and exits from any drawing room he visited, led most observers to believe that the wizard was providentially preoccupied by affairs of state.

Despite these personal obstacles, Suzanne, being maniacally diligent and virtuously in love with her husband (qualities not especially prized in Parisian society), succeeded in creating an important salon from which to launch the career of her "great man." She chose Fridays—the only day not currently occupied by another prominent *salonnière*—as her day to receive. And through sheer discipline and determination, by 1770 she had created a weekly gathering at which one could meet such luminaries as Diderot, Buffon, Gibbon, Holbach, and d'Alembert. As Sainte-Beuve would comment several decades later, Suzanne Necker had to totally "reshape her mind" to attain her social goals. The metamorphosis was not always easy. As hard on herself as she was demanding of others, she compensated for her lack of ease and esprit with arduous self-reprimands, constantly jotting down notes on how to improve herself. "One saw her busy making herself agreeable to her guests, concerned to receive properly, careful to say what might most please each person," wrote the author Jean-François Marmontel, a frequent guest at Suzanne's salons. "But it was all premeditated, nothing flowed naturally."[8]

The aura of Suzanne Necker's salon, in fact, was so calculated that one particular guest, a Chevalier de Chastellux, having once arrived a bit early to a gathering at the Neckers', found under an armchair a little notebook in which the mistress of the house had jotted down all that she must say to her most important guests: talk to a certain lady about love, discuss one particular author's latest book, instigate a literary discussion between two other literary gents. M. de Chastellux found the dinner delightful, having had the pleasure of "hearing Mme Necker say, word for word, everything that she had previously written in her notebook."[9]

So accomplished a hostess did she become, in fact, that Mme Necker's book *Mélanges,* published by her husband after her death, remains as instructive a manual of salon manners as any written in France on the eve of the Revolution. But Mme Necker's greatest gift to French culture was of a different order: she enjoined her little daughter, whose precocity she treasured, to attend all her salons, and even her dinner parties, on condition that she listen without speaking. And how well the child obeyed!

Chapter 2

Listening

Little Germaine, aged six, eight, ten, sits on a stool at the foot of her mother's armchair, listening to Diderot, or D'Alembert, or (just once, shortly before his death) Voltaire discourse on politics or human character. I imagine her sitting up very straight, her arms around her legs, her mouth slightly open in concentration. All onlookers were struck with the intensity with which this eerily observant child with curly black locks listened to adult talk. "It has to be seen how Mlle Necker listens! Her eyes followed the movements of those who were speaking and seemed to anticipate their thoughts,"[10] one memoirist wrote. "Her mobile features were so expressive that she did not open her mouth yet seemed to be taking her turn in speaking. She was aware of all, grasped everything, even political issues, which ... were one of the great themes of discussion."[11] The intense pleasure Germaine took as a child in the conversations overheard in her mother's salon had immeasurable impact on her literary career and decades later led her to muse in the following manner on the art of discourse:

> The feeling of satisfaction that characterizes an animated conversation does not much rely on

its subject matter—neither the ideas nor the knowledge that may emerge are of primary interest. Rather, it relies on the sense of . . . reciprocally and rapidly giving one another pleasure; of speaking just as quickly as one thinks; of spontaneously enjoying oneself; of displaying one's wit through all the nuances of accent, gesture, and glance, in order to produce at will a sort of electricity that causes sparks to fly, and that relieves some people of the burden of their excess vivacity and awakens others from a state of painful apathy.[12]

However, one should note that the joy offered Germaine by her immersion in adult conversations was just about the one delight of her youth. She was not a happy child. Her isolation from her peers, the glacial intensity with which her mother imposed a huge load of studies on her, the burden of overstimulation and under-socialization took its toll. Though Germaine's nature was radically different from her mother's—she was as warm, spontaneous, vivacious, forthright, and effortlessly brilliant as her mother was studied, rigid, and pedantic—she had inherited a few central traits of Suzanne Necker's character: a great capacity for self-dramatization, and an almost psychopathic hypersensitivity. Thus at the age of twelve Germaine had a serious nervous breakdown that manifested itself in alternating bouts of elation and deep despondency—a crisis that one might diagnose, these days, as an episode of manic depression. The doctors were wise enough to prescribe country rest, playmates of her age, and a measured detachment from her mother.

With resentful dignity, Mme Necker retreated from her daughter's life. Once Germaine recovered and returned to Paris, her education was given over to tutors and governesses.

The deep insecurity in Germaine's character that was at the heart of this episode, and that would later wreak havoc in many of her love affairs, was caused, in good part, by a lack of maternal affection. To do her justice, Mme Necker may have loved her daughter in her own demanding, self-centered way; but her manner was too cold and rigid to manifest her devotion, and she was incapable of responding to the emotions of a child who tended to express her needs with a terrifying intensity and vehemence. This lack of communication led Germaine to resent her mother for the rest of her life—an emotion further complicated by the totally extravagant passion she had for her father. Ever unrestrained in declaring her emotions, Germaine continued to claim, into adulthood, that her father was the love of her life, and that her greatest unhappiness was that she had not been able to marry him. "Of all the men in the world," she wrote in her journal in late adolescence, "it is him whom I would have wished for a lover."[13]

It may be that as Germaine came out of her depression she adulated her father all the more for his brilliant achievements, for his career was then at its peak. A year earlier Louis XVI had named Necker to be director general of finance, making him the second-most powerful man in France. The financier, during the time he held the post, made some highly intelligent, progressive reforms. He streamlined the method of tax collection; improved inmates' conditions in prisons and hospitals; abolished some four hundred ceremonial court appointments such as cup bearers and candle snuffers, all of whom received a government pension. Moreover, he had such great talent for raising loans that he was able to avoid imposing any new taxes or increasing existing ones, which made him a national hero to the French citizenry. In a most unusual instance of ministerial largesse, Necker not only refused a salary for his services but deposited 2.5 million *livres* of his own (approximately fifty million francs, 1990s vintage) into the pitiful royal treasury, at only 5 percent interest. (It would be over thirty years before his family got it back.)

No wonder, then, that Germaine had grounds to adore her father as a national genius, as well as cherish him as a companion. The passion was reciprocal. Necker, who had always adored his "Minette" (the nickname he gave Germaine in early childhood), enjoyed in her all the qualities absent in his wife. Minette cajoled him, flattered him, amused him, entered into all his preoccupations, and gave him a sense of youthfulness, freedom, and importance he had never found with Mme Necker. It was with her father, in fact, that Germaine learned to flirt, an occupation at which she would become exceedingly skilled. They teased each other a great deal—Necker called his daughter "Monsieur de Saint Écritoire," Mr. Holy Desk, because of her tendency to be constantly scribbling something. And Germaine modeled herself exceedingly on her father. Necker's easy, paternal manner with Louis XVI, for instance, to whom he spoke as a teacher speaks to a pupil, enabled his daughter, in later years, to be totally at ease with the many royals who needed her services (the one sovereign who did not, Napoleon, she addressed with a defiance that became legendary throughout Europe). Some would describe Germaine's love for her father as incestuous. But although he was indeed a principal love of her life, the keystone of their relationship was her total trust in a man whom the nation had already taught her to worship.

Germaine's filial adulation grew apace, out of anger and concern, in 1781, when Louis XVI dismissed Necker after the latter, in an act of sheer vainglory, had published a report on the nation's finances whose figures were transparently unrealistic and cosmeticized. His report, the *Compte Rendu au Roi,* served as cannon fodder for Necker's two most powerful enemies, chief minister Jean-Frédéric Maurepas and foreign secretary Comte de Vergennes, who had long been jealous of the king's reliance on Necker. They were all the more enraged by Necker's recent demand that he be given full membership in the council of ministers, a position thus far unheard of for a foreigner. They jumped on the opportunity offered by Necker's highly flawed financial report and persuaded the ever-vacillating king to dismiss the minister, threatening to resign if he retained him. Louis, ignoring the pleas of Marie-Antoinette, who is said to have spent the entire day weeping over her Swiss friend, invited the director general of finances to hand in his resignation.

The royal decision had long-lasting repercussions that would eventually be fatal to Louis XVI. From every corner of France letters poured into the Neckers' château at Saint-Ouen, ten miles from Paris, raging at the king's ungrateful treatment of his adviser and at the national crisis it would incur. The communications came from all members of society: nobles, bishops, peasants, soldiers, priests, and nuns. Most members of the court itself sympathized with Necker; princes of the blood and marshals of France traveled to Saint-Ouen to offer their support. By this time a powerful political faction had developed in France that enjoined Louis to accept a constitutional monarchy on the British model. For the next seven years, until his baleful recall in 1788, Necker would be looked on as a leader of that "pro-constitutional" opposition. "He is a man whom Heaven has destined beyond all contradiction to occupy the most glorious position in Europe," commented Russia's Catherine the Great, who from her distant kingdom kept a close watch on France's internal affairs. "His star will yet shine with incomparable brightness, and his contemporaries will be left far behind him."[14]

Necker's vainglory would have led him to agree wholeheartedly. But his eventual fall would come from a grave miscalculation. Because of his insatiable, narcissistic desire for the love of the French people, which had gone to his head, he was blind to the need for increased taxation, without which the national credit was bound to collapse. He placed his need for public adulation ahead of fiscal exigencies. This self-centered concern would eventually put an end to his career.

In 1785, at the age of nineteen, this is the way Germaine recorded her emotions about her father, who was then exiled in Geneva: "What grace, what charm he can display when he cares to . . . he wants me to love him like a lover while he speaks to me like a father . . . I wish him to be jealous of me like a lover while I act like a daughter."[15] Yet notwithstanding her adulation for Necker, Germaine would soon become too independent to be totally subservient to him, and eventually she would be able to be gently critical of him: "I adore my father," she wrote a friend when in her thirties. "It is a cult. But people do yawn at church."[16] And whatever her filial ardor, it is worth noting that the many men she was to love were strikingly different from M. Necker—almost all of them were unabashed roués. Straight-laced Calvinist virtue could never affect Germaine's conduct, as it had her parents'.

In 1784, during his first exile from the French court, M. Necker purchased a lovely manor house ten miles from Geneva, the Château de Coppet, a few hundred yards from Lake Leman, which has been associated with Mme de Staël ever since. Originally built in the fifteenth century, and restored in the seventeenth, it was, and still is, a light, airy, welcoming house surrounded by a beautifully wooded park, with a distant glimpse of the Alps. The house came with a title, an eighteenth century custom that pertained to many châteaus in Europe. Germaine's parents were now Baron and Baroness Necker.

Chapter 3

Loving

Mademoiselle Germaine Necker, aged sixteen, stands in front of a mirror in her bedroom, critically scrutinizing her reflected image, her anxiety heightened by the knowledge that her parents are busy finding a husband for her.[17] She is now quite tall, with a fairly slender waist, ample breasts, and unusually beautiful shoulders that she will display generously—sometimes shamelessly— for most of her life. She is only too painfully aware that she could not be called beautiful by any classical standard. Although her skin is admirable, and her large, luminous, hazel eyes would always be described, even by those who found the rest of her ungainly, as remarkable, her nose is a little prominent, her lips are too thick, her bodily gestures are sweeping, hurried, a bit gauche. And however praised and admired she is for her brilliance; her fluency in Latin, Greek, and English; her general wit, éclat, and charm, the sense of her own plainness would never leave her. "Madame de Staël would have given all of her intelligence for the pleasure of being beautiful," noted Mme de la Tour du Pin, one of the eighteenth century's most eloquent chroniclers, who added that Germaine's ardent love life may in fact have been dictated by her lack of beauty: she abandoned herself all the more easily to men, Tour du Pin opined, because "she felt pleasantly surprised whenever a man sought from her pleasures from which her unfortunate looks might have excluded her forever."[18] So Germaine would early gather some detractors, and it is her very brilliance that made her most controversial. "She is so entirely spoilt by the high opinion in which her intelligence is held that it would be difficult to make her perceive her shortcomings," another Parisian grande dame noted. "Were she not spoilt by all the incense burnt to her I'd venture to give her some advice."[19]

However devoid of most traditional aesthetic traits, Germaine had other major advantages as a potential bride. By her late teens she had mastered the art of conversation to a greater perfection than any of her peers, a skill that added immensely, in that century, to any woman's appeal. She had another important attribute, which was bound to be irresistible to many men: with a dowry of 650 thousand *livres*, she was France's wealthiest heiress, and one of the two or three wealthiest in Europe. She was bound to have attractive suitors, but she was picky. She turned down one of her first admirers on the grounds that such an alliance would force her to live too far away from her father: the frail but dazzlingly brilliant William Pitt the Younger, who would soon become, at the age of twenty-four, Great Britain's prime minister. The most persistent of her suitors was a Swedish nobleman, Eric Magnus de Staël Holstein; eighteen years older than she, he had begun negotiations with her parents when she was twelve, and he was the one who won out. Good-looking and elegant, with suave, polished manners, he had been a chamberlain to the king of Sweden, Gustavus III, and was noted for his bravery during the attempted coup of 1776, when a cabal of discontents had tried to overthrow the sovereign. So King Gustavus, who had appointed Staël to the Swedish Embassy in Paris, was cheering for his compatriot's union with Mlle Necker, as was Queen Marie-Antoinette of France, who loved to make matches and had a particular predilection for Swedes: her closest confidant, and perhaps her lover, was a Swedish nobleman, Count Axel de Fersen (reports of their degree of intimacy vary greatly).

If only by his allure, Staël had all the polish of the ideal courtier-diplomat: "*Faccia bella figura,*" Italians would have said of him. As a youth, moreover, he had endured the frugal, rustic life typical of ancient but impoverished provincial nobility, and the humiliation of early poverty had made him resourceful. He had entered military service at the age of thirteen, and, though barely educated, he was ambitious but not pushy, cunning but not devious. He had chiseled features, a shock of blond wavy hair, a slender, elegant body, and a blend of frivolity and cleverness that was then much in vogue in French society. As attaché to the Swedish ambassador to the French court, within a season he had acquired a good reputation in Paris and in Versailles. However, Staël suffered from one important flaw: an addict of the gaming table, he was very impoverished by his gambling debts and had remained desperate for the eight years the Neckers wavered about giving him their daughter in marriage. This weakness of Staël's gave M. Necker several additional aces up his sleeve and enabled him to set very tough conditions for the match. He let it be known to the king of Sweden that before he acceded to the union, Staël had to be made a full ambassador for life and also be given a title of nobility. The habitual haggling began: Gustavus III replied that he would offer Staël the ambassadorship and the title of Baron if Sweden could acquire a share of a certain French island in the Caribbean he particularly coveted, Saint Barthélemy. Under pressure from Marie-Antoinette, the French government acceded. Thus was the deal struck: Germaine was traded for a few hundred acres of what is currently the Caribbean's trendiest island.

It was not a time when brides had much to say about the marital arrangements brokered by their parents. Having adamantly turned down Pitt, Germaine despondently accepted Staël, who had made a mostly negative impression on her upon their first meetings, as he had on Catherine the Great of Russia, who looked on Staël as "a very poor match."[20] "I regret that I have not joined my fate to that of a great man, it is the only possible glory for a woman," Germaine noted about her groom. "Even his hand," she said another time, "seems made of white marble." "Monsieur de Staël," she also mused, "is incapable of saying or doing anything stupid and his conduct is perfectly correct, but he is sterile and inert. He will not make me unhappy, for the simple reason that he cannot contribute to my happiness. . . . M. de Staël is the only convenient choice for me."[21] Such was the morose attitude with which this young woman, who would become an addict of exalted romantic love, a proselytizer for challenging conventions, went to the altar.

The marriage contract was signed the evening before the actual wedding, at a small ceremony at the court of Versailles attended by the king and queen of France and all the princes of the blood. The following day the couple was married in the Lutheran chapel of the Swedish embassy. Among the small group of friends who attended the church wedding was Marie-Antoinette's friend Count Axel de Fersen, attaché at the Swedish embassy, who would later play a crucial role in the fate of the French monarchy.

After a few days spent, as custom dictated, at the home of the bride's parents, the newly married couple settled into the Swedish Embassy on the rue du Bac. Upon leaving her parents' house Germaine wrote a tearful letter to her mother, which is notable because she had seldom felt much affection for Mme Necker—the distress into which her marriage thrust her seemed temporarily to have deepened her devotion to her. "My dear Mama," she wrote, "This is the last day that I shall spend as I've spent all the days of my life. How hard it is to bear such change. I feel completely shattered and overwhelmed at this moment of parting from you. . . . In my new house I will no longer have a guardian angel to protect me from thunderbolts or fire. . . . " In closing she penned the following sentence, a fitting dictum for all victims of arranged marriages: "Happiness will come later; will come at intervals; may never come."[22]

M. de Staël's state of mind is not recorded in writing. But a year after the wedding, one close witness of the ménage, a secretary of the Swedish embassy, was of the opinion that "[Mme de Staël] loves and esteems [her husband's] character, but he loves her more."[23] Indeed, Germaine's future comments about her marriage, and later correspondence from M. de Staël, give the impression that it was Germaine, and not her husband, who withheld the tenderness and intimacy essential to a happy union. There is no reason to believe that she found the duties of the marriage bed distasteful, or that she refused to perform them—for the rest of her life she would look on sexual relations as an essential ingredient of deep friendship, and that emotion she certainly felt for her husband. Her first child, Gustavine (named after her godfather, the king of Sweden), the only one of her four children to be sired by Staël, was born a year after her marriage. Sickly from birth, in spite of her parents' tender ministrations the baby survived less than two years; Germaine seemed to bear her loss stoically, never mentioning it in her correspondence or writings.

So the central problem of the Staëls' marriage had little to do with sexual intimacy. It had to do with Germaine's inability to experience a true love devoid of intellectual and spiritual exaltation, and notwithstanding his many charming qualities, M. de Staël could not elicit exaltation in this most exaltable of women. Moreover, from the first months of their marriage, their social paths were vastly different and seldom crossed. Germaine continued to associate with the Paris literati. M. de Staël preferred the company of his Swedish friends, and that of his companion gamblers. There was only one purpose in life that truly united the couple: to restore the political power of Germaine's father, to whose destiny Staël had linked his. As one chronicler noted, this goal established between them "a certain conspiratorial intelligence and comradeship"; the Staëls' contact with each other was marked by "the affectionate cordiality reserved for old business associates."[24] There was another pivotal tension in the first year of their marriage that had to do, typically, with issues of fidelity. Germaine found it insufferable that her husband claimed liberties for himself—such as numerous extramarital trysts—which he did not permit her to indulge in. She found this double standard intolerable, and she remedied it very soon. Letting her husband know that he had no exclusive rights over her, highly aware of the fact that she held the purse strings, taking full advantage of her status as an ambassadress, she went out to seek happiness in Parisian society with magisterial independence.

On June 30, 1786, two weeks after her marriage, Germaine, Baronne de Staël, made her official debut into society by being presented at the court of Versailles. Her gown had been designed by the famous Mlle Bertin, Marie-Antoinette's own couturiere, who had strived to represent, in Germaine's garment, the genius of the bride's father, the virtue of her mother, and the already notorious candor of the bride herself. Germaine arrived a bit late, as was her wont, and began the ceremonial three curtsies; the tradition was that upon the third curtsy the lady being presented had to kneel before the queen, and kiss the hem of her dress. On that third curtsy, Germaine, quite clumsy by nature, stepped on her own train, lost her balance, and fell flat on her face to the floor. A gaggle of courtiers rushed to the throne to pick her up. They were joined by the kindhearted king, who gently said to her ,"If you cannot feel at ease with us, you will not feel with ease with anyone."[25] The incident caused a great stir; *le tout Paris* discussed the episode for the rest of the season. In her few weeks in society Germaine's outspokenness had already made her controversial. Her admirers commented on the good humor she had displayed throughout the incident, but those who already disliked her composed epigrams about her extreme gaucheness. It was clear that members of the Parisian elite, if polled, would have expressed more appreciation for the blandly polished Baron de Staël than for the forthright, bumbling young Baronne.

Perhaps as a way of allaying her marital frustrations, Germaine began to write more abundantly than ever after her marriage. Before she'd turned twenty-one she had written a tragedy, *Jane Gray,* and another play, *Sophie ou les sentiments secrets.* The latter work concerned a daughter's incestuous love for her father, and Germaine had the gumption to read it aloud to her parents, to their acute embarrassment. She earned her first notoriety as an author, however, through literary and social criticism rather than fiction, with her *Lettres sur les écrits et le caractère de Jean-Jacques Rousseau* (1788) in which, discussing the consequences of Rousseau's political ideals, she proclaimed her belief in an English-style constitutional monarchy.

Most significantly, it is through her salon, quite as much as through her writings, that Mme de Staël made her reputation as a brilliant woman of letters. No sooner had she settled into the Swedish Embassy on the rue du Bac than she upstaged her mother by creating the most dazzling salon in town. It was a very new kind of gathering, one suited to the aura of pre-Revolutionary unrest that had begun in the early 1780s. The literary stars of Mme Necker's drawing room—Voltaire and Rousseau—had died in the previous decade; the new luminaries of the 1780s were predominantly politicians. No more islands of pleasure-seeking suited to the exchange of elegantly phrased gallantries; salons were now dedicated to reforming France into a utopia of justice and to further weakening an already threatened monarchy. Moreover, as Mme Necker herself would note ruefully in those years, "One does not suggest playing a game of chess on the edge of a precipice . . . that flower of imagination, the last refuge of decency and delicacy, is lost in our political discussions."[26] Conversation had become openly critical of government, confrontational, conspiratorial. The financial deficit, above all the urgent need for a constitution—all issues relating to the restlessness of the French nation—were now the order of the day, and they were ideally suited to Germaine's temperament: "I have loved three things," she would say toward the end of her life, "God, my father, and liberty."[27] She forgot to mention one crucial predilection: conversation, which she looked on as the most important thing in life, next to love. She firmly believed that conversation is what the French missed most when they traveled abroad.

> Paris is recognized as the one city in the world where wit and a taste for conversation are most widespread; and what is known as the *mal du pays*, an indefinable mourning for one's country... is particularly applicable to the pleasure of discourse, which the French find nowhere to the same degree as at home.... All classes in France feel the need to converse: the spoken word is not only, as it is elsewhere, a means of communicating ideas, sentiments, and concerns, it is an instrument that is enjoyable to play and that, like music with some peoples and strong liquors with others, raises the spirits.[28]

Throughout the 1780s, Necker, dismissed by the king, had held unofficial court at his country house in Saint-Ouen, nine kilometers from the center of Paris. His tensions with Charles-Alexandre de Calonne, who succeeded Maurepas in 1785 as prime minister and inherited his predecessor's distaste for Necker, came to a head with the publication, that year, of Necker's three-volume treatise on the state of the French economy, *L'Administration des finances de la France*. Due to Necker's immense popularity with the French people, the work is said to have sold eighty thousand copies in a year. But Necker had formidable enemies in the king's entourage beyond Calonne, such as the Comte de Mirabeau and the Marquis de Condorcet. In February 1787 Calonne, addressing the Assembly of Notables that he had convened in an attempt to improve France's finances, threw a bombshell into Necker's camp by announcing that the former minister's earlier work, his *Compte Rendu* of 1781, which had shown a great surplus in national coffers, was a bunch of baloney: if rendered honestly, Calonne maintained, it should have shown a huge deficit. The humiliated Necker petitioned the king to make a public reply to Calonne's attack. The king, for once, was seriously provoked. "A plague on both your houses!" was his reaction. He refused Necker the permission to reply to Calonne and shortly thereafter dismissed Calonne himself. Necker published his reply without royal sanction, and his inflated ego led him to believe that the king would soon recall him.

This time he was wrong. Instead of recalling Necker, Louis XVI, miscalculating, as ever, the worsening crisis of his nation, sent him a *lettre de cachet* ordering him to leave Paris within twenty-four hours and to remain at a minimum distance of forty leagues from the capital ("an act of unprecedented despotism!"[29] Germaine exclaimed upon hearing of the king's edict). Within a few days, the vacillating monarch had softened and permitted Necker to stay at his estate at Marolles, near Fontainebleau, where he used to spend part of the summer months. Because the court was in Fontainebleau at that time, Necker had actually moved much closer to it. He had a delightful summer at his summer residence in the company of his wife and his daughter, who had had a social whirl the previous winter of 1786–1787, the first year of her marriage. She had spent the fall of 1786 with the court at Fontainebleau, where the king seemed to be either hunting or hearing mass (as Mme de Staël noted in a letter to King Gustavus III of Sweden, with whom she had started an extensive correspondence, when the court bulletin stated that "Today his Majesty is doing nothing," it meant that Louis XVI had spent the day working with his ministers). Germaine's life that season had been a succession of dinners and suppers: she'd visited three times a week with the Duchesse de Polignac, Marie-Antoinette's closest friend, and spent equal time with another royal favorite, the Princesse de Lamballe. And once a week she visited with the queen herself, who usually made her appearance at 11 p.m. to play billiards until the dawn hours. Though sharply critical of the emptiness of court life, Germaine missed its tumult, even its intrigues, in the solitude of her father's country houses. Above all she missed the man who may have been her first lover, the Comte de Guibert, whom she'd known since her early adolescence. Hippolyte de Guibert, a man twenty years her senior with literary ambitions (he was a member of the Académie Francaise), struck her as having many of her father's attributes: extreme sensitivity, ambition, love of glory—qualities she would always seek in a lover. And he was the first man who led Staël to throw a true fit of jealousy.

M. de Staël's reproaches about Guibert drew from Germaine an instantaneous reply. She would be delighted to show Guibert's letters to her husband to prove that there was nothing whatever between them! Staël read through the missives his wife handed him and immediately calmed down. Germaine had shown him only those letters that concerned the reproaches she had made to Guibert for having advised her, four years earlier, against marrying William Pitt the younger. Pitt had since become prime minister, and if Germaine were Mrs. Pitt instead of the Baronne de Staël, Germaine had chided Guibert in those letters, Louis XVI would never have dared subject her father to exile. M. de Staël was so pleased by these proofs of his wife's innocence that he agreed to plead Necker's case to the king of France. As a result, Necker's exile was revoked within two months, leading Marie-Antoinette to exult at her favorite's good fortune.

Chapter 4

Conversing

Germaine stands in her living room at the Swedish Embassy on the rue du Bac, her back to the fire, her hands behind her, twirling a small twig between her fingers (this habit allayed her overabundance of energy and she held to it all her life—whether she was in Paris, or at her Swiss home at Coppet, or abroad, her domestics would be on order to cut her a fresh twig of wood every day). She is generously displaying her shoulders, as is her wont, and is wearing a kind of taffeta turban on her head, partly because of her love for oriental styles, partly to make her abundant, wavy black hair more manageable (even under the ancien régime she often flaunted fashion by not wearing a wig). In the "Chambre Ardente," as her salon is known in Paris, she is displaying all the conversational brio, pliancy, and lightness her mother would have loved for herself but was never able to attain. Her comments, emitted in a fairly loud voice, with a precise elocution whose beauty was often praised, are always a theatrical performance, full of emotional intensity, and stated with electric enthusiasm; and they always concentrate on helping others to formulate their own feelings into words.

It was not in large assemblies that her powers shone most brilliantly: the smaller the circle, the more inspired her conversation, and those who knew her best agreed that she reached her greatest eloquence during tête-à-têtes. She started conversing as early as possible in the morning, during levees as public as those of the nobility under the ancien régime, holding forth to her guests as she was being coiffed, manicured, and laced into corsets. Be it in her boudoir or in front of her fireplace at the rue du Bac, her emotional intensity and intellectual mettle, the torrential sweep of her eloquence, the fiery enthusiasm with which she communicated her ideas led many Parisians to compare her sorties to dazzling musical performances.

And she seemed to grow on her audiences. An American diplomat who frequented her salon over a period of years, Gouverneur Morris, described her thus upon one of his first visits: "In the midst stood the hostess, in her favorite attitude before the fire, with her hands behind her back, a large, leonine woman, with few beauties and no grace of gesture. She nevertheless animated the salon by her masculine attitude and powerful conversation."[30] A few years later, in 1790, still an habitué of her salon, Morris described her as "a woman of wonderful wit and above vulgar prejudice of every kind," and her house as "a kind of Temple of Apollo."[31]

Although she talked a great deal, and even when not talking tended to leave her mouth slightly open, as if readying it for a riposte, Germaine was never accused of orating. Nor was she, as some of her critics have maintained, an incessant talker; she was just an extravagantly seductive one, and she lived at a time when eloquence was looked on as a central feature of any woman's attractiveness. Just as a prettier woman might snare men by playing up her physical charms, so Germaine—perhaps because of her plainness—had early learned to inflame them by the sheer power of language. Her tactics of seduction were far more complex than those of flattery and might be summed up in the following manner: Once she had discovered a vulnerable area in a man's sensibility—a particular field of interest, say, or a cherished avocation—she played to it with such adroitness that her victim was beguiled into sensing she might be the greatest confidante, the greatest muse he could ever find. And since her choice invariably fell upon men of great sensitivity, their sensuality was stimulated to a pitch that mere physical attractiveness never could have incited. In sum, like many a seductive *belle laide,* she had a genius for sensing what any one man needed to hear, for convincing him that he could not live without her, and for generally making him feel great.

Thus it was that this rather plain, sturdily built woman with admirable skin and eyes was able to lure just about any fellow she wished into her den. Thus it was that shortly before the Revolution she seduced, however briefly, a genius who deserves particular attention because he would have a deeper influence on his nation than any other man of Germaine's generation—Talleyrand.

Charles-Maurice de Talleyrand Périgord, the statesman notable for his perfidious deviousness, his sybaritic lifestyle, and his brilliant skill for political survival, came from an ancient, aristocratic family of limited financial means (he would manage to wheedle himself into high offices over forty years: during Louis XVI's last years, during the French Revolution, under Napoleon, under the restoration of the Bourbon monarchy, and in the 1830s under Louis-Philippe). As an infant he had been shipped out to a nurse in a Paris suburb, where he was said to have fallen from a chest of drawers, causing permanent injury to his foot. Because this infirmity prevented him from following the family tradition of an army career, his parents groomed him for the church. He took his first mistress while still a seminarian, was ordained at twenty-five, and began his career as a court cleric. Described as having "an angelic face animated by a diabolical spirit,"[32] he spent more time at Versailles with the fashionable wits and beauties of the day than with other men of the cloth. Talleyrand's brilliant role as the head of the Assembly of the Clergy, in which he valiantly managed to raise the living standards of the humbler country priests, led him to acquire a reputation of great astuteness; and in November 1788, on the eve of the Revolution, he was appointed by Louis XVI to be the bishop of Autun. His own mother was the first to protest this advancement—he was only thirty-four—because of his noted profligacy.

As bishop of Autun, Talleyrand was one of the clergy's delegates to the Estates General, the legislative body which had not met since 1614 and in which the three orders of society (nobility, clergy, and Third Estate) had traditionally been represented separately. At the opening of the Estates General at Versailles in May 1789,

Talleyrand immediately attracted vast attention and acquired great influence, eventually becoming one of the National Assembly's more radical deputies. He succeeded in lobbying for the adoption of the Civil Constitution of the Clergy, a series of measures that, to the profound horror of the Vatican, completely reorganized the French church on a democratic basis. He would be the first bishop to take the oath of loyalty to this Constitution and would be immediately excommunicated by the Pope, which, since he had already been planning to leave the Church, did not in the least distress him. The maverick statesman simply resigned his bishopric and thenceforth dedicated himself to his duties as a secular deputy to the National Assembly.

In private life Talleyrand was the quintessential indolent, hedonistic grand seigneur. A man of middling height, with an upturned nose and a habitually haughty and insolent expression, he walked with a severe limp; he made up for his physical shortcomings with extraordinary wit and charm. A noted bon vivant, he enhanced the middle years of his career by hiring the great chef Carême and flattering visiting heads of states with the most epicurean hospitality in Paris. Even though his rapacity was noted throughout Europe—he shamelessly solicited bribes from numerous foreign governments in exchange for preferential treatment—his seductive powers were such that he never fell from grace. ("He would sell his soul for gold," Mirabeau once quipped about him, "and he'd be right, for he'd be exchanging dung for gold."[33]) Yet Talleyrand, who was often referred to as "the limping devil," combined cynical self-interest with a highly developed literary sensitivity and, upon occasion, with a great sweetness and delicacy of demeanor that were irresistible to both genders. His two closest friends were Auguste de Choiseul, whose uncle had served as prime minister to Louis XV, and Louis de Narbonne, a high-ranking noble with powerful connections at the court. Noted for their libertine ways and their numerous conquests, this triad of men was at the heart of Paris's most fashionable circles. It is probable that Germaine de Staël first met Talleyrand at court in the winter of 1788–1789; after what seems to have been the briefest of trysts, their friendship lasted for decades. Some kind of initial fling there must have been, for toward the end of her life Germaine declared that the three men she had most loved had been her father, Talleyrand, and Narbonne. In this kind of raffish high society it would have been typical for men to pass their lovers on to each other, and it is the thirty-three-year-old Narbonne, introduced to her by Talleyrand, who in the winter of 1789 became Germaine's next lover.

Chapter 5

Romancing

Vicomte Louis de Narbonne was seven years Germaine's elder. His preeminent qualities—handsomeness, intelligence, sensitivity, and a fine reputation as a seducer—were made all the more alluring by the mystery of his origins. He was said to have been born in Italy to a Comtesse de Narbonne Lara, whose husband was conspicuously absent when the infant was baptized at Versailles; there Madame Adelaide, Louis XV's daughter, had stood as his godmother, and the future Louis XVI as his godfather. Madame Adelaide would remain ardently protective of Narbonne until the end of her days, which led many to suspect that he was her own child, the issue of an incestuous relationship she had had with her father, Louis XV. Whatever the true nature of his origins, Narbonne was brought up at court with the princes of the blood. He readily acquired the Bourbons' gambling habits, and by the age of thirty he had squandered Madame Adelaide's fortunes as well as those of his own wife, with whom he had made a loveless marriage of convenience in 1787. Because of his quasi-royal lineage, he was given an entire regiment to command "without ever having fought a battle except on sofas and beds,"[34] as one chronicler of his time put it. Far handsomer than Talleyrand, Narbonne possessed the same refinement of charm and manner as his close friend and was infused with a genuine idealism that the sardonic Talleyrand could never have possessed. Due to his royal connections he initially did not see eye to eye with most members of Mme de Staël's salon, many of whom belonged to the liberal aristocracy that was about to carry out the first phase of the Revolution. But in time Germaine's own high ideals and eloquence convinced him to join their ranks, and espouse the cause of a constitutional monarchy.

By the last months of 1789 Germaine's affair with Narbonne was public knowledge. And by December of that year she was pregnant by him, having shrewdly flattered her husband into thinking that he was her future child's father by fulfilling her marital obligations at strategic moments. Auguste, born in August 1790, was the first of the two sons she would bear to Narbonne and would be the more brilliant and successful of them.

Germaine's first grand passion, and the birth of a child she would deeply love, occurred during the most tumultuous moment of French history—the Revolution of 1789. The events of the preceding year had set the stage for the uprising: even nature had conspired to make the years 1788–1789 the harshest in French history. The hailstorms of July '88 had ravaged wheat crops and caused the price of bread to soar. The winter of 1788–1789 had been the coldest in eighty years. Thomas Jefferson, the American envoy in Paris, reported that forty-thousand workers were unemployed that season in Normandy alone. The Paris Parlement, which had called for the Estates General to meet the following summer, had refused the king's proposal to levy a new stamp tax, declaring that only the Estates General could take such measures. Throughout the winter and spring there were numerous uprisings throughout France, and the collection of taxes became impossible. It is in the context of these upheavals that Louis XVI recalled Necker in November 1788, offering him the post of comptroller general and the powers of a prime minister. Although he had no concrete plans for tackling the monumental problems France faced, Necker's vanity led him to accept the cabinet position, which he'd awaited for years, and which had only recently been made possible by the abolition of earlier taboos against foreigners in the king's ministry. "The public's joy in this change of administration was very great indeed,"[35] he wrote later with typical self-satisfaction. He went on to enact some unimpressive stopgap measures, raising enough loans to keep the administration going over the winter, and doing everything in his power to ensure the good fortunes of the Third Estate in the forthcoming meeting of the Estates General. But the more astute political thinkers saw the situation as being beyond remedy. Even Germaine, notwithstanding her immense faith in Necker's abilities, had predicted that the state of the nation was too dire to save. "He has been given a vessel so close to shipwreck," she wrote to the king of Sweden, "that all my admiration for him is barely enough to inspire me with confidence."[36]

In May 1789, Germaine, standing at a window at Versailles, watched the twelve hundred deputies of the Estates General make their solemn procession to a mass held in their honor on the eve of their first meeting. Following the royal couple came the Swiss Guard and a group of mounted royal falconers, each with a hooded falcon attached to his wrist. There followed the twelve hundred deputies walking in solemn procession: the three hundred prelates and priests in their sumptuous robes; the three hundred nobles bristling with plumes and swords; the heralds who accompanied the nobles, dressed in purple velvet, mounted on white steeds, and blowing silver trumpets. Germaine was particularly struck by the six hundred members of the Third Estate—"men of letters, merchants, a great number of lawyers," as she described them—whose simple black coats contrasted with the satins and gold lace of the nobility: She especially noticed the ravaged, pockmarked features of the powerful Mirabeau, who was one of the few nobles to have been elected as a deputy to the Third Estate and was considered by many to be a traitor to his class. "His huge head of hair distinguished him from everyone else," she noted. "It was as if his strength derived from it, like Samson's. His face gained in expressiveness from its very ugliness, and his whole person suggested a strange power."[37]

The following day, in an improvised structure erected over the main avenue of Versailles, the king and queen, sitting on a dais, officially opened the meeting of the Estates. Tellingly, members of the Third Estate did not kneel when they came into the royals' presence. Germaine observed the weakness and melancholy engraved on the face of the king, whose white beaver hat was set with a huge diamond. The queen looked unwell, agitated, and deathly pale, evidently despairing over the imminent death of her son, the eight-year-old dauphin. On that long-awaited day, much was expected from Necker's address to the National Assembly: all hoped he might inaugurate a new era of democratization for the monarchy. But Necker lost his last chance of saving his adopted nation: his speech was a disaster. He droned on, citing figures and statistics exclusively on the topic of taxation and the public debt, and after half an hour his voice gave out—the rest of his two-and-a-half-hour speech had to be read for him. The only aspect of his oration the deputies listened to with pleasure is that no new taxes would be needed if the "proper measures" were taken. The principal reality left out of Necker's speech—and most of the delegates were aware of it—was that the nation's coffers were empty. From that day on, Necker's popularity at the National Assembly became volatile at best.

In the following weeks the deputies' attention concentrated on the following issue: should the three orders—nobility, clergy, Third Estate—vote separately, the majority of each order constituting one vote, or should the votes be counted by heads? In the former case, the first two orders were assured of a permanent majority of two to one; in the latter case, the Third Estate was favored. Liberals like Germaine and, to a more reluctant degree, her father, were in favor of the latter alternative; they also hoped that the Third Estate would propose, and the king would accept, a bicameral constitution modeled on the English system. The Neckers' aspirations, and those of their milieu, were clearly utopian: there was little chance that a constitutional monarchy *à l'anglaise* would find favor with the royal family.

Soon after the opening of the Estates General, Necker committed another serious gaffe and further demeaned himself in the public eye. In hopes of creating a stronger alliance of centrist candidates who could help steer a middle course between reaction and revolution, mutual friends of Necker's and Mirabeau's decided to arrange a meeting between the two men. So far the two had had a low opinion of each other. Mirabeau, like his colleague Lafayette, had a clear view of Necker's limitations and of his political ineptitude. Necker had a prissy distaste for Mirabeau's racy reputation, which indeed fell deplorably short of Calvinist standards. The meeting was arranged. As Mirabeau came into the financier's presence, Necker assumed his most disdainful and chilly air. "Well, sir," he said, "[I am told] that you have some propositions to make. What are they?" "My proposition, sir, is to wish you a good day,"[38] Mirabeau replied, turning around and leaving the room.

Necker's superciliousness sealed his fate. After rejecting Mirabeau's alliance, a nobler trait of his character—his blunt honesty—led him to alienate whatever influence he still enjoyed at court. Having warned the king that popular opinion ran overwhelmingly in favor of the Third Estate and that the army had become unreliable, he was icily dismissed from the palace by the Queen and the Comte d'Artois, the king's youngest brother, who three decades later, as Charles X, would become one of French history's most inept and reactionary rulers. The following night, June 22, 1789, Necker decided not to attend the Estates General meeting, a decision that clearly signaled his opposition to the King and briefly redeemed him in the eyes of the delegates and the citizenry.

A famous episode followed: The king, having made his speech to an icily hostile audience, left the room where the Estates General, soon to be known as the National Constituent Assembly, were meeting. When the king's master of ceremonies announced Louis's order to disperse the Estates, Mirabeau thundered in reply, "Go tell your master that we are here by the will of the people and shall not yield except to the force of bayonets!"[39] A day later, M. Necker was recalled to the palace, where the continually vacillating royal couple begged him to retain his post. Necker, having agreed to remain minister, was returned to his lodgings carried on the shoulders of a clamorous crowd. Germaine would always remember this event with the greatest joy. "All those voices repeating my father's name," she would recall two decades later, "seemed to be those of a crowd of friends who shared my respectful love."[40]

In the following crucial weeks, a rumor spread that the king's more conservative advisers had convinced him to surround Paris and Versailles with twenty thousand men, to attack the National Assembly. On July 10, 1789, reacting to Mirabeau's protest against the massing of the troops, the king replied that they were merely meant to maintain public order. The following day the faltering king had another change of heart concerning Necker. As the minister was about to have dinner with his family and a few friends in his quarters at Versailles, one of the king's attendants announced himself and handed him a letter. After briefly perusing it, Necker put it into his pocket without a word to his dinner companions. It notified Necker yet once more of his dismissal (for the third or fourth time? One loses count) and ordered him to leave the country instantly and discreetly—*sans bruit*, "without noise." Apart from squeezing Germaine's hand a few times, he showed no sign of distress. Once dinner was over and Germaine had left for Paris, Necker and his wife, still in their dinner clothes, summoned their carriage and were driven at highest speed to Brussels, where they arrived the following day. Soon after his departure, Germaine received a note from her father, which advised her to go to his estate at Saint-Ouen to avoid public reprisals. She prepared to leave, but within a few hours the news of Necker's dismissal became public. "Delegations of citizens from all areas of the city," Germaine recalled some years later, "addressed me in the most exalted language on the subject of M. Necker's departure, and on what I should do to force his return."[41] On the mornign of July 13, she received another note from her father informing her of his whereabouts. Summoning her husband, for once, to her side, she immediately left for Brussels. She was in such an emotional state that upon entering her father's quarters she threw herself at his feet.

While in Brussels, Necker demonstrated his fidelity to France by renewing his offer of two and a half million *livres* to the French nation. As one historian of the epoch has commented, this is the only recorded instance of an ousted finance minister donating a major part of his fortune to the country from which he's fled—the opposite process is usually the rule.

After the briefest of family reunions—a few hours— Necker and M. de Staël proceeded quickly to Basel. Germaine and her mother traveled more slowly. It is only when the two couples were reunited in Basel some days later that they heard about the fall of the Bastille on July 14. Parisians' reaction to the news of Necker's dismissal had been tumultuous. Green cockades—the color of Necker's livery—had immediately appeared on people's hats. Images of Necker had been paraded, held aloft, through the city's streets. All theaters had closed, as if in a token of national mourning. On July 13, two hundred thousand people had marched on Paris, calling out his name. The following day, the mob stormed the Bastille, murdering the fortress's governor, the gentle Marquis de Launey, and liberating its seven remaining inmates, which consisted of four forgers, a libertine nobleman, and two lunatics, one of whom was certain that he was Julius Cesar.

In the last week of July, shortly after the Neckers had received news of the Revolution, yet another messenger arrived from Louis XVI to—guess what? Recall Necker for the umpteenth time. This time Necker had serious doubts about whether to accept. His wife, who was suffering from worsening bouts of neurasthenia and was increasingly addicted to opium, was staunchly opposed to his returning to Paris. Germaine was adamantly for it. His vanity once more prevailing, he accepted his daughter's counsel.

That journey from Basel to Paris was one of Germaine's most blissful moments: "The enthusiastic acclaim of an entire people accompanied his every step," she would recall later, "my father's carriage pulled along by the citizens of each city we crossed, women working in the fields falling on their knees as his carriage passed by. . . . Nothing ever offered me as powerful an emotion."[42] The ovations greeting Necker reached their climax in the square facing the Hôtel de Ville, where a huge crowd had gathered to greet him. "The entire population of Paris crowded the streets. One saw men and women on windows and on rooftops crying out '*Vive M. Necker!*'"[43] Germaine would always recall this as "the strongest impression and the last truly happy day" of her life. The power of that ecstatic moment, she tells us, led her to faint—the first of many swoons of delight, despair, and ecstasy that would fell her in the next decades.

A few hours later Necker was greeted with rapturous applause at the National Constituent Assembly, whose members were once more expecting the Swiss genius to save a France plagued by anarchy: her army was disintegrating, her coffers were empty, citizens in all provinces were rebelling against an impotent king. But once again, in yet another startling instance of political ineptitude, Necker blew it. Instead of calling for a meeting of the cabinet to agree on a course of action, which is what the Assembly was waiting for him to do, he decided to issue a plea for clemency for a highly unpopular Royalist general, a fellow Swiss called Pierre-Victor de Benseval, who had spent his life in the French army. Benseval, whose hands were already bloodied by having shot down groups of insurgents, had been in charge of the troops Louis XVI had ordered massed around the city and had recently been captured by rebels. Necker's blatantly unseemly action—pleading for an unpopular compatriot's life, when France was on the verge of collapse—alienated him once and for all from the French citizenry. It even lost him the support of the masses, the only power base he had still maintained. Now ignored by the Assembly, more and more distrusted by the king and queen, increasingly isolated, as unable as the monarch of devising or following a firm plan of action, he managed to hang on to his post for another thirteen months, until August 1790, when he was forced to quit a final time.

Chapter 6

Surviving

Germaine is seated at her desk at the Swedish embassy, writing letters, on October 5, 1789. She is all too aware that tensions between the monarchy and the French nation had grown to unprecedented heights the previous month, when the king had refused to sign the Declaration of the Rights of Man. On this October morning, she is suddenly brought word that a large mob of Parisian citizens, alarmed by predictions of another winter of famine, is marching on Versailles, led by thousands of women determined to confront the king and demand their bread. M. and Mme Necker are already at Versailles, spending the week in an apartment in a wing of the palace reserved for France's ministers of finance. Germaine immediately orders her carriage and by taking small secondary roads manages to arrive at the palace before the Parisian hordes, by taking small secondary roads.

It was already dark when the irate marchers, soaked to the bone by an icy rain, reached Versailles, at which gate they settled in noisily for the night. At midnight, after a hasty examination of the scene, General Lafayette gave the king his habitually rosy report: The troops remained loyal, he reassured the monarch, the demonstrators appeared calm, everyone should go to bed. He retired, as did the Neckers, whose apartments were connected to the palace by a long corridor. But the night's events contradicted all of Lafayette's fatuous predictions. In the predawn hours an elderly noblewoman of the queen's entourage rushed into Germaine's room: "She informed me that assassins had broken into the queen's quarters, and had massacred a few of the guards posted at her door," Germaine later recalled, "She had only been able to save her own life by fleeing through the secret stairs that led to the king's quarters."[44] M. Necker had already hurried to the king's side; Germaine alerted her mother, and the two women hastened after him. Upon exiting the corridor that connected their apartment to the royal quarters, they saw large pools of blood on the floor. They hurried on into the Grand Salon, where the Court was gathered, waiting for the queen. Below, in the courtyard, the mob was shouting for the king to return to Paris, "traditional home of your ancestors." As Marie-Antoinette entered the salon, composed but anxious and dreadfully pale, the Neckers learned that the bed she left a half hour earlier had been slashed to pieces by members of the Parisian hordes, who thought she was hiding underneath the mattress. Now loud cries came from the courtyard, beckoning the queen to appear at the balcony. Marie-Antoinette calmly went out, holding her children by the hand. "No children!" the crowd shouted. The queen took the children back to the Grand Salon and went back to the balcony alone. Her valor seemed to soften the crowd; there were some acclamations, followed by an encore of the earlier chorus, "The King to Paris!"

Upon leaving the balcony, Marie-Antoinette turned to Mme Necker and, suppressing her tears, said: "They will force us, the king and me, to go to Paris, with the heads of our bodyguards carried before us on the points of their pikes."[45] Her prediction was not totally accurate. The heads of the slain guards were kept out of the royals' sight while the king and queen were brought back to Paris, accompanied by members of the Assembly and by the boisterous mob. The Neckers traveled separately in their coach, by way of the Bois de Boulogne. Once in Paris, the royal family was ordered to change their home: they would no more live at the Louvre, but in far smaller quarters that were easier to guard—at the Tuileries.

Back in Paris, Germaine and her friends still saw a chance of consolidating the Revolution's accomplishments while keeping it from a more radical course. The king had finally signed the Declaration of the Rights of Man, the Constituent Assembly was drafting a constitution that limited the king's power; for the time being, enough had been accomplished to create a more democratic France. Necker had bumbled his way out of any significant power, and the nation was now under Mirabeau's guidance. Mirabeau had transformed the entire financial structure of the country by nationalizing émigré property and that of the church, and issuing money in the form of *assignats*— paper currency covering the value of the confiscated lands. In July 1790 Necker reached the nadir of his career

when he capitulated to the Assembly's demands for yet
another report on his financial administration. The data
he submitted showed a surplus of ninety-nine million—a
patently absurd figure for the destitute nation. This time,
the obvious inanity of Necker's report incited a series
of demonstrations against him from all sectors of the
population. On September 2, 1790, a mob marched on
his office, shouting threats of burning it down. Lafayette,
one of many in the royal entourage who had been jealous
of the king's confidence in Necker, immediately took
advantage of his bête noire's weakness. He sent him a
government carriage, and a bodyguard of six hundred
men, with the suggestion that the Neckers save their
skins by leaving Paris as soon as possible. The Neckers
slipped away to Saint-Ouen that very same night, and a
few days later left for Coppet, whence the Minister sent
in his final resignation. He would spend the rest of his
days in his native Switzerland. Seldom had the mighty so
suddenly fallen.

Germaine, who had just given birth to her oldest child,
Auguste, followed her father to Coppet a few weeks later,
as soon as she felt her infant son was ready to travel.

What about the cuckolded husband, Swedish Ambassador Magnus de Staël? He was now more penurious than
ever, his gambling debts having grown to unprecedented
proportions. He was also out of favor with his king,
Gustavus III, who suspected him of anti-Royalist
sympathies. Moreover he was engaged in an utterly
ridiculous romance. He had taken a fancy to an actress
thirty years his senior, Mlle Clairon, who was approaching

seventy and who, by an eerie coincidence, was the same Mlle Clairon who had served as drama coach during Germaine's childhood. Playing on Staël's despair and on his intense need for mothering, Clairon had somehow managed to make him sign a paper that awarded her a substantial yearly pension. Staël was involved in yet another folly: he had joined a particularly mystical form of the Swedenborgian sect and was busy conjuring spirits. Such involvements would not have been seen as outlandish by Swedes, who since early medieval times had dabbled heavily in sorcery and occult practices. King Gustavus himself and his brother were surrounded by soothsayers, and Staël had long retained at his embassy a Swedenborgian who specialized in making spirits appear in mirrors (he particularly favored the image of St. John the Baptist). But in this instance Staël's standing with the king of Sweden was weakened by the fact that his particular Swedenborgian mentor was also a Freemason, the member of a group that believed that the French Revolution was "the divine deed par excellence, the most solemn deed ever witnessed since the Deluge . . . nothing less than the Day of Judgment for the tyrant."[46]

Germaine remained disdainfully aloof from her husband's mystical excesses and his absurd romance. She was far too obsessed with her own love affair with Narbonne, with her general dedication to causes of freedom and justice, and with her particular goal of guaranteeing civil liberties in France to pay attention to a bumbling husband whose career was foundering in debt and mysticism. So preoccupied was she by liberty and love that she did not even seem to have been crestfallen by her father's downfall. In fact, she seemed relieved that he was now in full safety in Coppet. Back in Paris, she was enjoying, both in and out of her salon, the comradeship of the increasingly powerful Talleyrand; the love of Narbonne, for whom she was planning a brilliant political future; and a semi-amorous friendship with one Mathieu de Montmorency, a highly progressive young aristocrat who had actively worked to strip his own caste, the nobility, of its traditional privileges. Tall and slender, elegant and refined, ablaze with the most altruistic ideals, Mathieu must have embodied, in Germaine's eyes, the most precious qualities of the sector of society she sought out most eagerly—the liberal French aristocracy. Mathieu and Germaine would remain lifelong friends.

In September 1790, Germaine reluctantly left for Switzerland with her newborn son to join her parents in Coppet. Although literary history would always link her name with Coppet, and although it would serve as a precious refuge during her future exiles, she never liked the place. She found the landscape uninspiring, and Swiss society desperately conservative and dull. When, years later, the great writer Francois de Chateaubriand visited her at Coppet and praised the beauty of her estate, she replied with a sigh: "Ah! The gutter of the rue du Bac!"[47] The atmosphere at Coppet was particularly difficult at the time she reached it in October 1790. Her father had not begun to resign himself to his fate; he spent his days deploring the infidelity of royals, and in the words of one visitor, Mme Necker's old friend Edward Gibbon, was "the most miserable of human beings."[48] As for

Germaine's mother, her opium addiction had irreparably impaired her mind.

The arrival of thousands of French citizens fleeing the Revolution made it even harder for the Neckers: the émigrés held the former minister responsible for their tragic fate. Moreover, the Genevese themselves had for decades watched the Neckers' fortunes with a blend of envy and derision and had disliked the couple for their aura of grandeur, which made them unpopular among the dogmatically egalitarian Swiss. As for Mme de Staël's mores, they contradicted every possible principle of Calvinist propriety. The Genevese's distaste for Germaine was fully reciprocated. "I shall confess to you that the society of the Genevese is unbearable to me," she wrote her husband. "Their love of equality is but a desire to drag everybody down; their liberty is insolence, and their morality is boredom."[49]

For a few weeks Germaine, terribly irritated by Geneva, went to stay in Lausanne with a Madame d'Arlens, a cousin of Benjamin Constant, the prominent essayist and novelist whom she was to meet three years later and who for many decades would play a central role in her life. There is a fine portrait of the twenty-six-year-old Germaine written by Mme d'Arlens during that stay:

"She is an astonishing woman. The feelings to which she gives rise are different from those which any other woman can inspire. Such words as sweetness, gracefulness, modesty, desire to please, deportment, manners, cannot be used when speaking of her; but one is carried away, subjugated by the force of her genius. It follows a new path; it is a fire that lights you up, that sometimes blinds you, but that can not leave you cold and indifferent." And yet, Germaine's hostess added, "It is astonishing to find in this singular woman a kind of childlike good humor which saves her from appearing in the least pedantic."[50]

All those who knew Germaine well stressed this outgoing, good-humored, *bon enfant* quality that strikingly contrasted with her mother's character. But she was hardly satisfied by the affection of some Swiss friends. A few days after her visit to Lausanne Germaine left the "infernal peace" of Coppet to return to the celestial din of Paris.

Chapter 7

Lobbying

Upon returning to Paris in the winter of 1790–1791 Germaine set herself a new task. Only one leader, in her opinion, could consolidate the gains of the Revolution and transform them into a constitutional monarchy, and that leader was her lover, Narbonne. She and her lover stood for progressive centrism and sought to block the rise of fanatics on the left and on the right. The tortuous negotiations that Germaine used to have Narbonne appointed minister of war would be worthy of the wiliest D.C. lobbyist of our time. One must admit she had good material to work with: Narbonne was far more enterprising and astute than the more illustrious Lafayette; Napoleon himself would declare, decades later, that Narbonne had been one of his ablest diplomats. Germaine was only able to get Narbonne appointed by turning her salon into a forum for all shades of moderate opinion: from left of center circles she cultivated the company of Jean-Paul Brissot, an influential deputy to what would now be called the Legislative Assembly, and of the Marquis de Condorcet, a famous mathematician and physicist; from the other, more conservative end of the spectrum, she sought the support of equally influential deputies, Antoine Barnave and the Lameth brothers. Her own triad of intimates—Talleyrand, Narbonne, and Mathieu de Montmorency—held less influence in the inner councils of the Assembly than the men above, but their independence was admired.

Because of her adamantly moderate stand, Germaine soon became anathema to the extreme right and the extreme left, which, however irreconcilable they were on any other issue, united in unleashing venomous sarcasm against her. In the writings of the Royalist pamphleteer Rivarol, she appears as "the Bacchante of the Revolution," and, in an allusion to her rather masculine appearance, the only person in Europe "capable of deceiving the public about her gender."[51] In another pamphlet, "The Intrigues of Mme de Staël," she is depicted as a nymphomaniac who stirs up riots to keep her lovers. Yet another ditty, satirizing her attempts to unite disparate political parties, shows her as receiving the Royalists in the morning, the Girondists for dinner, the Jacobins for supper, "and everybody at night."[52]

The major event that nullified all the efforts of Germaine's milieu, and sealed the fate of the French monarchy, occurred on June 22, 1791, when the royal family made its ill-fated attempt to flee to Belgium. There were many motives in Louis XVI's decision to escape from France, but the principal one was his religious conscience. He was a truly devout man and could not bear to abide by the Civil Constitution of the Clergy, which divided priests and bishops into those who refused to take the civil oath (many of whom left France for exile abroad), and those like Talleyrand who took the oath and had been excommunicated by the Vatican. Louis could not tolerate the thought of hearing Mass said, of being confessed by, of taking communion from, an excommunicated priest. And he also yielded to those conservatives in his milieu who were pressing him to join the émigré aristocrats abroad. The escape plan of June 1791, which was minutely choreographed by the queen's great friend, the Swedish diplomat Count Axel de Fersen, was a perfectly good one; it aimed to take the royal family to the town of Varennes, some two days northeast of Paris, on the frontier of the Netherlands, where a large contingent of foreign and Royalist troops would whisk them to safety across the border. But the plan failed, through a chain of unfortunate coincidences: Marie-Antoinette delayed the departure by an hour by losing her way in the dark halls of the Tuileries; above all, the outlandish size of the Berline coach, which the king had insisted on because he wished to travel with all members of his family, was far too conspicuous. The failure of the attempted flight, which led Fersen to write to Gustavus III, "Sire, all is lost," was a tragedy for the monarchs. Escorted back to the capital by thousands of irate citizens and soldiers, met by contingents of national guardsmen who had crossed their rifles in midair as a sign of defiance, they reentered the city amid a silent, hostile crowd of thousands. The king's bungled escape opened a new page in the course of the revolution. Shortly after his return to Paris, it was discovered that in recent months Louis had written a letter to his cousin the king of Spain in which he disavowed the reformist decrees he had been compelled to sign since 1789. Along with the botched evasion, this document eroded whatever love or respect the French still had for their monarch and deepened the split between the country's moderate and radical factions. From this time on, the royal family would live like captives.

The Varennes debacle also made it far more difficult for Mme de Staël to press the cause of Narbonne's accession to the Ministry of War. By this time the low esteem in which the royal couple held Lafayette and Mme de Staël—the two had become the royals' nemeses— would have made the nomination impossible. They only acceded to it because the right-of-center deputy Barnave, who had recently gained great influence with Marie-Antoinette, was persuaded by Mme de Staël and the Marquis de Condorcet to praise Narbonne to the queen; Barnave convinced Marie-Antoinette that Narbonne's experience and military prestige could help to save the monarchy, and Marie-Antoinette, solely in deference to Barnave, persuaded the ever-vacillating king to make the appointment. On December 6, 1791, Narbonne was installed at the War Department. On December 7, he addressed the Legislative Assembly and received enthusiastic acclaim. Meanwhile, the queen, seeing through everyone's game, bitterly wrote to her favorite correspondent, Comte de Fersen: "At last Narbonne is minister of war. . . . What a triumph for Mme de Staël, what pleasure to have all the army at her disposal! [Narbonne] might be useful . . . since he is clever enough to rally the Constitutionals, and [has] just what is needed to speak to the army of today."[53]

What glory, indeed! Within a month, Narbonne had 150,000 troops stationed at the frontiers. He then departed to inspect them in the company of Mathieu de Montmorency, a close friend of his and of Germaine's. The soldiers heartily cheered the new hero and his flamboyant speeches, and a new aura of confidence settled over the country. Yet war seemed imminent. In January 1792, a group of Assembly delegates proposed that unless Austria disavowed the Declaration of Pilnitz, which called on Europe to restore Louis XVI to his throne, France would declare war. The declaration of war came on April 20 and began a conflict that would last, on and off, for some twenty-two years, and cost the lives of millions of soldiers without bringing an ounce of additional liberty to France.

As for Germaine's triumph in having Narbonne appointed to the Ministry of War, it was short-lived. His alliance with the Girondists had already made Louis XVI suspicious of him, and Germaine's pleas to enhance his importance by making him foreign minister made Louis dislike him all the more. She took another false step: she persuaded Lafayette, Rochambeau, and other ministers to write letters begging Narbonne to remain at his post and threatening to resign if he was dismissed. The king learned of the stratagem and banished Narbonne. This was one of the few times Germaine showed herself to be vindictive: she prevailed on influential statesmen such as Condorcet and Brissot to topple the entire cabinet.

Brissot, in fact, accused the foreign minister, Comte de Lesant, of high treason for having negotiated with the Austrian emperor. The accusation was unanimously endorsed by the cabinet, Lesant was arrested, and the rest of the cabinet resigned. Germaine's triumph was a bitter one. The royal couple was all the more set against Narbonne and Lafayette. In her book *Considérations sur la Révolution française,* Mme de Staël devotes only two brief pages to Narbonne's rise and fall from power and never mentions her role in it. Since humility was not one of her distinctive traits, she seems to have realized that this was one maneuver she had botched.

By now it was clear that Gustavus III was looking on himself as Europe's principal champion for the divine right of kings, and that he was deeply concerned about the fate of Louis XVI. In June 1791, right after the royal family's botched attempt to escape, he ordered his ambassador to extend all possible aid to the French royal couple and admonished Staël to avoid any action "that would compromise your person or your dignity."[54] Staël obeyed only in part, closing his embassy on the rue du Bac to social functions, which forced Germaine to hold her salon in Necker's home or at Mme de Condorcet's. But M. de Staël continued to praise his wife's lover, which was more than Gustavus could tolerate. Early in 1792 Staël received his final recall. With the intent of dealing directly with his monarch, who wished to break off all relations with France, Staël set off for Sweden. He landed on March 12. On March 16, at a masked ball, Gustavus was shot to death by the same group of conspirators that had tried to kill him a decade earlier, when Staël had proved his valor by saving his monarch's life. (The later, fatal attempt against Gustavus is immortalized in Verdi's opera *Un Ballo in Maschera.*)

To Staël's relief, Gustavus was succeeded by his young son, who would reign as Gustavus IV; Duke Carles de Sudermania, a good friend of Staël's, was assigned to act as regent for the boy king. One of the first decisions the regent made was to order Staël back to Paris as ambassador. Not eager to return to the Terror beginning to rage in France, Staël dallied some months in his native land. As he lingered in Sweden, his wife was witnessing the escalation of the Terror. On June 20, 1792, a large mob armed with hatchets and pikes moved upon the Tuileries, where, unopposed by the National Guard, they made their way into the royal apartments. Demanding that the king's veto power be abolished, they jeered and jibed at the royal family, making threatening gestures and forcing the king to put on the red bonnet that symbolized Republican liberty. Germaine's description of the mob—as usual, she rushed over to the Tuileries as fast as she could to witness the events—exemplifies her marked distaste for France's have-nots.

> 20,000 men of the lowest class of society armed with pikes and lances marched on the Tuileries with no reason in mind.... Their physiognomies were marked by that moral and physical coarseness which would even inspire disgust in the most philanthropic-minded. If they had been animated

by some genuine grievance, if they had come to protest against injustice, against the high price of grain, against the increase of taxes, against military conscription—in a word, against all that power and wealth causes the poor to suffer . . . then everything about them would have aroused pity. But their frightful oaths and shouts, their menacing gestures, their murderous weapons, offered a horrifying spectacle which could forever destroy the respect which the human race should inspire.[55]

The mob was not that different from the one that had held her father on their shoulders the previous year, and that she had so lauded. "You will soon hear all the details of the insults imposed on the King,"[56] Narbonne, who deeply loved his royal kinsman, wrote to General d'Arblay. Furious at the insults leveled at Louis XVI, and determined to safeguard him, Narbonne left his troops on the northern border and came to Paris to seek justice from the Assembly, demanding that those who had taken part in the insurrection be punished. Despite the queen's hatred of her because of her leading role as a constitutional monarchist, Germaine, who had been equally appalled by the mob's treatment of the monarchs, now devised her own plan of escape for the royal family, one she thought would have a better chance of success than Fersen's ill-fated Varennes venture. (As Talleyrand once quipped, Germaine delighted in drowning people to have the pleasure of fishing them out again.) Her scheme was the following: She would buy an estate in Dieppe, and in the company of her son Auguste, who was the same age as the Dauphin, she would travel there several times in the company of a man and a woman who resembled Louis XVI and Marie-Antoinette as closely as possible. Once the patriots had seen this retinue a few times, the royals were sure to pass when they impersonated their previous stand-ins. From Dieppe a small ship would quickly carry them to England. Narbonne was to drive the coach, as Fersen had the previous year. Lafayette approved of the plan and offered his help. The stratagem may indeed have been more foolproof than the previous one. But the queen, who was still gambling on the possibility of a French military victory, and who hated Germaine, Lafayette, and other liberal Constitutionalists as much if not more than the Jacobins, refused even to receive the emissary sent by Germaine to propose the new escape scheme.

A few weeks later, on July 14, 1792, when the fall of the Bastille was once more celebrated on the Champ de Mars, Germaine was there again, this time scrutinizing the royal couple. "When he climbed up the stairs of the altar," she wrote prophetically about the King, "he looked like a saintly victim offering himself up for sacrifice."[57] It would be the last day, Germaine noted in her *Considérations sur la Révolution française,* that the French people saw the king in person before he went to the scaffold.

Chapter 8

Safeguarding

A dramatic new escalation of the Terror occurred several weeks later, on August 10, 1792, a day often referred to as "The Second Revolution." This time the stakes were raised by a powerful new group of radical insurgents called the "sans-culottes," so called because of their contempt for a potent class symbol—the *culottes,* or knee breeches, traditionally worn above the silk stockings of bourgeois and nobles. Primarily artisans and small shopkeepers, the sans-culottes had so far been denied most forms of political emancipation: they had not even been allowed full membership in the Assembly, which required a certain level of income and was initially restricted to the most educated middle class—jurists, doctors, men of letters. (It was the sans-culottes who outlawed the traditional Monsieur and Madame forms of address and imposed the familiar *tu* on all classes of society.) On August 10, after invading the Tuileries and massacring the king's private guards, a frenzied group of sans-culottes went on to raid the homes of many nobles, including Germaine's friend Stanislas de Clermont-Tonnerre, whom they murdered in a particularly savage way, throwing him from a window and dragging his mutilated body back to his wife.

On the morning of the August 10 uprising, upon learning that her compatriots, the Swiss Guards, were being massacred at the Tuileries, Germaine hurried into her carriage to witness the events first hand. When she arrived to the bridge that crossed the Seine—the Tuileries were close to the opposite bank—her carriage was stopped by guards who, with brutally explicit gestures, signaled that on the other side of the river persons in her kind of coach were likely to have their throats cut. The royal couple, she also learned, had been moved from the Tuileries to the Temple, a former monastery of the Knights Templar that now served as one of Paris's most rigorously guarded prisons. Germaine, who had hoped to offer her support to the king and queen, retreated to her home and within a few hours began to hear reports of the day's barbaric events, which included the murders of over one thousand prominent aristocratic citizens, or "aristos" as the sans-culottes called them. In the following days, the Assembly voted to abolish the institution of kingship. It named an executive council, which was guided by Robespierre, an accomplished jurist, and his acolyte Saint-Just. They were appointed to rule until a new elected legislative body, the National Convention.

From then on Germaine, protected to a degree by her Swiss citizenship, courageously devoted herself to saving the lives of as many Constitutionalists as possible. In the following days she would hide Narbonne and their mutual friend Mathieu de Montmorency under the altar of the Swedish embassy's chapel. Soon thereafter she arranged for Narbonne's passage to England, having rented a country house in Surrey, through the intermediary of the half-British Duchesse de Broglie, to serve as a shelter for her French acquaintances. With the help of an influential member of the Commune, Pierre-Louis Manuel, who dabbled in literature and was flattered to be petitioned by Paris's most eminent literary woman, she also obtained the release of two other close friends, Francois de Jaucourt and Trophime de Lally-Tollendal, who had been imprisoned the previous month. She was prescient to take all these measures: the massacres that occurred the following month would be the bloodiest to date. Some four weeks after the August 10 massacre, hordes of sans-culottes forced their way into several Paris jails, indiscriminately murdering women and children along with aristocrats, common criminals, and "refractory" priests who had refused to take an oath to the Civil Constitution of the Clergy. One of the mob's victims was Marie-Antoinette's closest friend, the Princesse de Lamballe, whose barbarically disfigured head would be paraded at the Temple before the jail cells of the former monarchs, now referred to as Citizen and Citizenness Capet.

It was at the end of that bloody August week that Germaine, six months pregnant with Narbonne's second child, left Paris to join her parents in Switzerland. She chose to travel in her grandest "berline" coach, with her postilions and servants in full livery, thinking that she would thus be less suspected of leaving the country. But her gambit did not work. As soon as her carriage lumbered into the Paris streets, hordes of toughs and "women issued from hell,"[58] as she described them, seized her coachmen: she was eventually ordered to drive to the Hôtel de Ville, the headquarters of the Paris Commune presided over by Robespierre. "Surrounded by an armed mob, I made my way through an arch of pikes," she later described the event. "As I mounted the stairway, which was also bristling with lances, a man pointed his weapon at my heart . . . Had I stumbled at that moment, it would have been the end of me."[59] The assembly she had been taken to was passing judgment on dozens of citizens. Just before Germaine's turn came, as she was preparing her oration on diplomatic immunity, the friendly Commune official Pierre-Louis Manuel appeared and whisked her, along with her chambermaid, into his office. The two women were there for six hours, still not knowing their fates. From the window Germaine could see "the murderers returning from the prisons, their arms naked and covered with blood, shouting horrible screams."[60] The charitable Manuel had to wait until nightfall to liberate the women; after handing them two passports, he escorted them back to the rue du Bac. Early in the morning, an emissary of the Commune arrived to take Germaine to the closely guarded Paris toll gate. He was Jean-Louis Tallien, a relatively centrist member of the Commune's governing board, who two years later would play an important role in overthrowing Robespierre and liberating France from the thralldom of the Terror. After the Paris toll gate Germaine was free to roll on to Coppet, which she reached four days later. By the time she entered her parents' home and fell (most certainly weeping) into her father's arms, over 1,360 prisoners, including forty-three children, had been butchered in Paris alone.

By September 7, when Germaine arrived at her home in Coppet, the Jacobins were preparing a revolution of their own in Geneva. Coppet, only five miles away, did not feel safe to the Neckers, and they quickly moved to a friend's home in Rolle, some thirty miles up the shore of Lake Leman. Notwithstanding the reassurance she always felt in her father's presence, Germaine's mood was desperate: her entire life now revolved around Narbonne. She had only one thought in mind: to join Narbonne in England as soon as her child was born. She even told her parents that she wished to divorce her husband to have her freedom, a step that her parents vehemently opposed. Necker kept reminding his daughter, with no great effect, of the privileges offered by her status as ambassadress, and how these would be threatened by making her liaison with Narbonne so public. But Germaine would not be swayed. She loathed Switzerland too much ("Here I am in this hole of Rolle,"[61] she wrote Narbonne) to survive there more than a few weeks. She kept repeating that for her, it was "either England or the bottom of the lake."[62] Family disputes with her parents continued, with increasing bitterness. The priggish Mme Necker, as well as her husband, were riled by their daughter's second pregnancy—by this time Germaine had not seen her husband for ten months and could not pretend the child was his. Germaine was all the more anguished by the fact that Narbonne's letters were extremely infrequent. So Germaine's techniques of emotional blackmail, at which she would become increasingly skilled with her future swains, went into high gear (the absent or evasive lover is her executioner, stabs her through the heart, drags her to the scaffold of the torture wheel, leaves her to die in a desert or at the gates of hell itself). Careless about maintaining any pride, totally devoid of any tact, she resorted to threats of suicide, to threats of traveling to England though eight months pregnant—if she or her child would die of it, it would be Narbonne's fault.

The house Germaine had rented for Narbonne and other endangered friends, Juniper Hall, was at Mickleham, Surrey, and Narbonne was there in the company of a whole colony of French refugees who were mutual friends of his and Germaine's. They included Mathieu de Montmorency, Francois de Jaucourt (whom Germaine had sprung from jail with Manuel's help), his mistress Mme de Chartre, and the high-ranking French military man, General d'Arblay. Talleyrand, who was living in London with his mistress—she had taken to making straw bonnets to support the couple's meager finances—was a frequent visitor. The French émigrés, financed to the last meal by Germaine, lived comfortably though not extravagantly. They were well received by the British and quickly made friends with their more glamorous neighbors, who included the Locks of Asbury Park—friends of Joshua Reynolds and of the late Dr. Johnson—and Dr. Burney and his two daughters, Fanny Burney and Susan Phillips. Seemingly oblivious of their poverty and uncertain future, the French émigrés jested, argued, played parlor games with a verve that dazzled their British friends. But however hard they tried to keep up their spirits, the French colony could not help but be obsessed by news of the events in France. In late 1792 two events particularly haunted them: the king had been put on trial for his life, and a law had been passed advising all émigrés that their property would be seized if they did not return to France. Narbonne, a devoted and loving kinsman of Louis XVI (he was, after all, his godson, and perhaps his half-brother), was terrified by the possibility of his cherished relative being put to death. He called on Pitt to intervene on behalf of Louis, with no success, and he offered to return to France to testify in person at the king's trial (a dangerous and futile step, because the Jacobins judging Louis had put a price on Narbonne's head).

Germaine's second son with Narbonne, Albert, was born at Coppet in November, and she was still recovering from childbirth when she heard of Narbonne's offer to return to France to testify for the king. He had no right to torture her so, she wrote him! What she was intimating, with the outlandish arrogance and self-centeredness she would display in most affairs of the heart, was this: What right had he to risk his life, which she had saved, for the sake of his cousin, the king? Heedless of the familial ties that bound her lover so strongly to Louis XVI, she insinuated that Narbonne would have done better to mourn the victims of the September massacres.

As for Germaine's own plans, they focused exclusively on "England or the bottom of the lake!" She kept repeating the phrase to her parents, oblivious to their reminders about the enormous dangers she would run when traversing Terror-stricken France. Her father predicted she would be murdered by brigands; her mother accused her of deserting her children and breaking her father's heart. "England or the bottom of the lake!" she continued to exclaim. A few days before Christmas she wrote Narbonne: "The moment has come to choose between you and the rest of the universe, and it is to you that my heart compels me."[63] Fibbing to her parents (she told them she was making a brief visit to Geneva), she left for England soon after the New Year and arrived at Juniper Hall in the third week of January. On the same day she arrived—January 23, 1793—the guillotine fell upon Louis XVI's neck.

Germaine had expected expansive displays of affection from Narbonne, or at least some share of the passion she felt for him, and was deeply chagrined by his gloom, his sorrow over the death of the king, and his emotional blankness toward her. She was far too self-centered to sense the extent of his grief and the deep-seated reasons for it. As Fanny Burney put it, this man whom she'd characterized as having "the highest character for goodness . . . sweetness of manners, and ready wit," had been "annihilated"[64] by the news of the king's execution. As for his relations with Germaine, he had tried every possible tactic and argument to keep her from coming to Great Britain. But such was her energy, her willpower, and the force of her eloquence that like many of her future lovers he had neither the courage nor the power to put an end to the affair. Dignified and grave, upon her arrival he offered her no more than aloof courtesy. One can imagine the extent of her disappointment and wrath.

But for a while Germaine made the best of a bad
deal and quickly won the affection of other residents of
Juniper Hall, and of its British neighbors. She particularly
captivated the affections of Fanny Burney, who described
Germaine as "one of the first women I have ever met
with [such] abilities and extraordinary intellect."[65] As
for Burney's sister, Susan Phillips, she had a startlingly
accurate insight into the relationship between Germaine
and her lover Narbonne. "Their minds ... ought to
be exchanged, for he is as delicate as a really feminine
woman and evidently suffers when he sees [his mistress]
setting proprieties aside, as it often enough befalls her
to do."[66] Another friend of the Juniper colony, Erich
Bollman, a young German doctor who had spent much
of his life in France and whose sympathies were strongly
with the constitutional monarchists, wrote of Germaine
during her stay at Juniper Hall: "The Staël woman is a
genius—an extraordinary, eccentric woman in everything
she does. She sleeps only a few hours and spends the
rest of the time in uninterrupted and furious activity. She
spends one-third of her day writing, even while her hair
is being dressed or while she is having breakfast."[67]

Germaine was indeed engaged in writing a book at
Juniper Hall, her first original work. It was entitled *De
l'Influence des passions sur le bonheur des individus et des
nations*. A large section meditates with great poignancy
on the impossibility of women—especially exceptional
women—achieving true satisfaction in both love and
work, and its many passages on female unhappiness
were surely reflections of the despair she experienced

over Narbonne's vanishing love. Its most famous passage, in fact, is an apology on suicide, which she had probably written in Switzerland just before she left for England, when her spirits were at their lowest. She read chapters of the book to the assembled company as soon as she had finished them, and they were judged by Fanny Burney to be "truly wonderful for powers both of thinking and expression."[68]

By the end of the year, however, the initially idyllic relations prevailing between natives and exiles at Juniper Hall began to fray. Horace Walpole disapproved of unmarried couples and refused to receive Germaine and Narbonne, or Jaucourt and Mme de la Châtre. And Dr. Burney warned his daughter that Mme de Staël's morals were not to be emulated by any proper British lady. The forty-year-old Fanny Burney was affected by her father's advice and, terrified of losing her pension from the queen, refused all further invitations to Juniper Hall. "Your sister is like a girl of fourteen,"[69] Germaine quipped to Fanny's sister, chagrined by the loss of the friendship.

In the spring of 1793 the existence of the Juniper colony was further threatened by events on the Continent. In February, France had declared war on England and the Netherlands, and a few weeks later on Spain. In May, after the defeat of the centrist Girondin Party, the Terror in France escalated. By the end of that month, Germaine capitulated to the pleas issued by her father and by her husband, who had resumed his ambassadorial post in Paris, that she return to the Continent. Germaine now had a new plan for handling her private life: She would go back to Switzerland, where both Staël and Narbonne would join her in a pleasant ménage à trois. She even offered that Narbonne be "absolutely free" in this relationship, which the decorous nobleman wanly agreed to at first, to avoid yet another lovers' dispute, but which he was far too proper to fully accept.

So Germaine left tearfully for Coppet, having extracted a promise from both Narbonne and Talleyrand that they would soon follow her there. At Berne, just before reaching Geneva, she was met by her husband, whom she had not seen for over a year. And at Coppet she was reunited with her children Auguste, now three years old, and Albert, seven months. Both were far more familiar with their grandparents than with their mother. And although she would eventually become an exceptionally devoted and beloved parent, for the time being "The Mother of the Gracchi,"[70] as Germaine often dubbed herself (referring to the legendary brothers who were democratic leaders of early Rome), had too much on her mind to give her offspring her full attention. She was preoccupied, above all, with Narbonne's reluctance to join her in Switzerland, and by his silence. She again pleaded with him in letters that displayed the most groveling kind of emotional blackmail. She ran a fever, she was ready to kill herself because of his heartless treatment of her, her "suffering would even invoke Marat's pity."[71] A few months after she had left Juniper Hall, a few evasive letters began to appear from Narbonne, and she slowly had to reconcile herself to the waning of his love.

Yet even in the throes of romantic agony Germaine continued her courageous project of rescuing political victims. In the fall of 1793 she focused her energies into composing a defense of Marie-Antoinette, who was scheduled to appear before the Revolutionary Tribunal, where she would have to endure the same kind of show trial her husband had undergone the previous January. It did not matter to Germaine that the queen had hated her—she was not one to bear grudges. She identified her as a woman who was being subjected to the cruelest kind of sexual slander, and as a foreigner who was being used as the traditional scapegoat. So she went about composing a defense of the queen, *Réflexions sur le procès de la Reine*. Appealing directly to the emotions of "women of all countries, of all social ranks," she drew a poignant contrast between the elated reception Marie-Antoinette had received when she first arrived in France, "young, beautiful, combining grace and dignity,"[72] and her present state as a grieving wife and mother, loathed and defenseless. Even though she published the pamphlet anonymously, it was a hazardous text to have written. It was immediately seized and destroyed in France, and it caused great difficulties for both Staëls. A few weeks after Germaine's defense of the queen had been issued, a posse of soldiers descended on the Swedish embassy, where, despite the Staëls' diplomatic immunity, they impounded all of the Swedish ambassador and ambassadress's papers. It was only thanks to the embassy chaplain's repeated complaints to the French Foreign Ministry that the papers were eventually restored.

Germaine's pleas for clemency for the queen were no more successful than Narbonne's had been for the king. Marie-Antoinette's head "fell into the basket," as the expression of the times went, on October 16, 1793. Among the most noted of the twenty or so people a day who went to the scaffold in the weeks after the late queen's execution were the King's cousin, the Duc d'Orléans (who during his term as a radical deputy to the National Convention, where he voted for his own cousin's execution, had called himself Philippe-Egalité) and twenty-one Girondin deputies, among them the valiant Mme Roland.

Meanwhile, back at Coppet, Germaine remained busy on two fronts: the more pathetic one was her fruitless struggle for whatever remained of Narbonne's love. "I cannot bear it any longer," one letter reads. "May my cries, my terrible despair, soften your heart. I'm ashamed that I haven't yet put an end to my miserable existence, but how can one die if there is a hope of seeing you again? And your children! Have pity on them and me. Save me, save me!"[73]

Such was Germaine's psychic energy that the sorrows of thwarted love did not keep her from expanding her rescue operation: it is one of the more extraordinary ones in recent history, equal in scope to the Scarlet Pimpernel's. It aimed to whisk numerous French citizens onto foreign soil to avoid the Terror. Among the dozens of lives she saved were those of Narbonne's former mistress Madame de Laval; the mother and the wife of Mathieu de Montmorency; the Princesse de Noailles; the Duchesse de Broglie; the Princesse de Poix. Her system was simple enough: She paid Swiss men and women, specially selected to resemble the people they were rescuing, to travel to Paris, where they would hand their passports over to the French citizens waiting for them; those endangered persons would then cross the border into Switzerland with legitimate-looking, forged papers. As for the Swiss rescuers, they could claim that they had lost their papers, and the border guards never gave them any problems. "There is no greater possibility of happiness than to save the life of an innocent person,"[74] Germaine wrote in later years. And it is in this "traffic in human flesh,"[75] as she called it, that she most clearly revealed her altruism and greatness of soul. It was an expensive operation: passport forgers and Swiss impersonators asked high fees; one rescue alone could easily cost 40,000 livres.

By summer 1794, when Narbonne finally reached Switzerland, Germaine's heartbreak over him had healed: she had recently embarked on a new liaison with a handsome Swede, Count Adolf von Ribbing, who had led the plot against Gustavus III a decade earlier, and whose original death sentence had been commuted to perpetual exile. To Narbonne's immense surprise, Germaine met him with mild affection and no reprimands. And though long out of love with her, he was annoyed to find himself so handily replaced. He resumed his former affair with Mathieu de Montmorency's mother, Mme de Laval, and the two couples spent a few fairly harmonious months at Germaine's Swiss home. Although Germaine, with ever-exaggerated delusions of grandeur about herself, thought the men were fiendishly jealous of each other, Narbonne and Ribbing actually struck up a good friendship. One morning, the two men were seen leaving the château together at dawn. They had argued the previous evening, and Germaine fell into hysterics, convinced that they had gone off to fight a duel over her (a notion that, of course, greatly flattered her). To her surprise, the two men reappeared at dinnertime in fine spirits, carrying a basketful of fish they had caught together in Lake Leman.

It is also at this time that Germaine was taken with one of the strangest ideas that would ever cross her mind: Talleyrand, expelled from England under the Alien Bill of 1792, had refused Germaine's invitation to follow her to Switzerland and had instead opted to leave for America. Germaine suddenly decided to follow him there. She bought 38,000 acres in upper New York state, and she even wrote Talleyrand to ask him if he thought Philadelphia might be a suitable diplomatic post for her husband. But it was an impulsive notion, incited by her deep friendship with Talleyrand. The thought of moving to America left her mind in a few weeks: there was no possibility of a new diplomatic post for M. de Staël, who, more bankrupt than ever by the yearly stipends he had pledged to pay Germaine's former drama coach, Mlle Clairon, and his even greater gambling debts, continued to find his chief solace in Swedenborgian mysticism.

At Coppet, Germaine had another family duty to take care of: the death of her mother, in May 1794. The loss did not cause her undue sorrow, but she was much concerned about her father, who was inconsolable about his wife's death, and most dutiful about embalming her, as she had long ago willed it, in a tubful of alcohol. The death of Suzanne Necker's first love, Edward Gibbon, had preceded hers by four months.

Meanwhile, in Paris, the Great Terror that marked the months of June and July 1794 had begun. More than one thousand people were executed in the seven weeks that preceded Robespierre's downfall (on 9 Thermidor, or July 27, 1794), which was precipitated by a coalition of right- and left-wing deputies who agreed on little else but the need to depose the tyrant once known as "The Incorruptible." In the months that followed Robespierre's demise and the end of the Terror, Germaine longed for nothing but to return to Paris ("I hold all of Switzerland in a magnificent horror,"[76] she wrote her husband, and "Better dead in Paris than live in Switzerland!"). There was still too much to be done to safeguard her friends, Robespierre's passing not having stopped the Jacobin Convention's reprisals.

It is toward the end of Germaine's magnificent rescue operation that she met the man whose destiny would be intertwined with hers for the rest of her days—Benjamin Constant.

PART II

Exile led me to lose the roots which had bound me to Paris, and I became a European.

　　　　　　　　—*Madame de Staël,* Dix années d'exil

Chapter 9

Benjamin Constant

It would be a grievous understatement to say that Benjamin Constant, the Swiss-born writer who was about to enter Germaine's life, had had a difficult childhood. His mother died a few days after he was born. During his early years his father—a cold, distant, cynical army officer—placed him in the care of his housekeeper. Unbeknownst to the boy the housekeeper was also his father's mistress and had borne him two children. From the age of eight, young Constant was shipped out to various relatives—aunts, cousins, grandmother—in towns as diverse as Lausanne, Brussels, and Edinburgh. And he was assigned a startling variety of eccentric tutors, few of whom could keep up with Constant's amazing precocity—at seven he was fluent in Greek and an accomplished pianist; by the age of twelve he had already written a tragedy in verse. One tutor took the boy to live in a bordello; another alternated beating him and smothering him with kisses; and yet another mentor, a defrocked monk called Duplessis, committed suicide. There followed two years of study in Germany, where Constant became fluent in the language; he then entered the University of Edinburgh, whose splendid faculty included Adam Smith, and where he may well have spent the two happiest years of his life. But his father ordered him back to France and placed him once more in the care of tutors; upon hearing that one of them had given his ward a very active tour of Paris's whorehouses, however, Constant père gave his son a small stipend to live in Brussels or Paris on his own. By this time the nineteen-year-old Constant was a confirmed gambler; had learned to respect no one and distrust everyone; and impressed those who met him as an arrogant, sharp-tongued cynic, the pose he had devised to mask his considerable sensitivity. His first love affair, with a warm, maternal matron unhappily married to a Genevese husband, was an idyll whose serenity he vainly sought to re-create the rest of his life. There next came a noted bluestocking beauty some twelve years his senior, Mme de Charrière, also known as Belle Van Zuylen (the "Zélide" of Boswell's diaries). Opinions differ as to their physical intimacy, but this nervous, agitated, brilliant woman, who was the first to introduce Constant to opium, served as an excellent finishing school for his sentimental and intellectual education and also nursed him tenderly during his first serious bouts of bordello-induced syphilis.

Benjamin Constant's physique hardly compensated for his irascible, contentious character. He was indeed one of the oddest-looking men of letters of the times: gangling, stooped, very pale, with red-rimmed eyes and a head of startling carrot-hued hair. While in Germany serving as chamberlain to the Duke of Brunswick—a position his exasperated father had obtained for him in hopes it would reform him—Constant inexplicably fell in love with one of the Duchess's ladies-in-waiting, Wilhelmina Von Cramm, who was ugly, short-tempered, impoverished, and passionately intent on getting married. But she offered Constant some of the affection and maternal solicitude he so craved, and he married her a few weeks before the outbreak of the French Revolution, in May 1789. He was then twenty-two years old. Six months later he had grown totally indifferent to her, and between his returns to Mme de Charrière he was courting a sweet, pretty young matron who even divorced her husband—at about the same time Constant was divorcing his own ugly wife—in hopes of marrying him. By then Constant's employer, the Duke of Brunswick, had become fed up with the young man's shenanigans and fired him. At the age of twenty-seven, the former child prodigy had to admit to himself that so far, he was a total failure. Here is how he described himself, that year, in two introspective moments.

Blasé about everything, bored with everything, bitter, self-interested. Endowed with a kind of sensibility that merely tortures me, unstable to the point of passing for mad . . . how do you expect me to succeed, to please, to live?[77]

Another time:

I am tired of my own persiflage, tired of surrounding my heart with a joyless atmosphere of indifference

which deprives me of the sweetest sensations . . .
to this fatal wisdom. . . . I prefer the madness of
enthusiasm.[78]

It is at this critical time in his life, in the summer
of 1794, that Constant met the supreme enthusiast
of his time, Germaine de Staël, about whom Mme
de Charrière had very negative opinions: she had met
Germaine the previous year, and, offended by her
forthrightness, referred to her as "the talking machine."
Moreover, her wit was pretentious, Mme de Charrière
complained, and her morality was doubtful. "Perhaps
she has taken Catherine II of Russia as her model,"[79] she
once suggested. But Constant seems to have disregarded
Charrière's warnings.

It was an equally opportune time for Germaine to
meet Constant. She had finally resigned herself to the
loss of Narbonne's love and was seeking, as she put it, to
"begin life anew, minus hope."[80] Recent political tragedies
had equally depressed her: the Terror that followed the
French Revolution had shattered many illusions she had
previously held concerning liberty and fraternity.

There are several versions of the circumstances in which
Germaine and Constant first met, but the most common
is the following: On a summer morning, Constant, who
was staying nearby, was seized by a great desire to meet
the famous woman of letters and cantered to her house at
Coppet to seek an introduction. He was told that she had
left an hour earlier to go to Lausanne. He galloped on
the road to that city, caught up to her carriage, stopped

her horses, and introduced himself. She invited him into her coach (it is not recorded what he did with his horse) and they talked for the next twelve hours. Constant, for whom conversation was a central joy of life, was yet another man felled by Germaine's dazzling eloquence; that first journey was the prelude to what may be the most loquacious love affair in the history of literature.

Shortly after meeting Germaine, Constant wrote his former mistress, Mme de Charrière, that he had met "a being apart, a superior being such as one might come across once in a hundred years, a being [so extraordinary] that those who are close to her... need not demand any other happiness."[81]

Mme de Charrière answered him with admirable straightforwardness. "Love her! Get enthusiastic! You're free to do so, just as I'm free to write to you no longer."[82]

It is hard to think of another man whose sexual advances Germaine rejected more adamantly than she rejected Constant's. However captivated she was by his wit, however impressed with the genius of his intellect, he repelled her physically as no male had before (he was "as appetizing as a freshly dug-up carrot,"[83] she quipped). Admittedly, his predecessors—the elegant, idealistic Narbonne; the handsome, incisive Count Ribbing; the sensitive, brilliant Chevalier de Pange, whom she would vainly try to seduce until his premature death in 1796— were hard acts to follow. As for Constant, he must have been rather vexed when he first arrived at Coppet. The house and its environs had become a refuge for many male acolytes of Germaine's, all of them Constitutionalist

Royalist émigrés who did not yet dare reenter Parisian life. So Constant found himself to be merely one of many admirers under her roof. The reason he soon gained an exclusive place in his hostess's life is that she instantly recognized his intellectual talents and took him on as her literary and political collaborator. Germaine, with her usual delusions of grandeur, was planning to reenter the political scene by uniting right-of-center and left-of-center factions behind the Republic, and by mediating a peace between revolutionary France and the European powers that were trying to topple its new regime. These were also Constant's ideological goals at that time. The first pamphlet they were to collaborate on, *"Réflexions sur la paix intérieure,"* was initially printed in a small publishing plant run by their friend Francois de Pange.

But Constant was not satisfied to be an honored colleague. Soon after meeting Germaine he firmly decided that he wished to become her lover. Madame's response was adamant: friendship yes, love no. So Constant played for her body in his usual, melodramatic style: Soon after he landed at Coppet, in the middle of the night the house was filled with shouts and moans clearly traceable to Constant's quarters. Some of the numerous houseguests—in their nightgowns, candles in hand—rushed into his room and saw an empty bottle of opium on his bedside table. He was dying, Constant moaned, and wanted to say a final adieu to his hostess. Germaine was alerted. "You wretch! What have you done?" she cried out when she reached his bedside. "Call a doctor!" she commanded one of her servants. "Ah, it is

you," Constant moaned, "It is for you that I perish. . . . "
"Live, Monsieur Benjamin, live,"[84] she whispered. He
seized her arm and covered it with ardent kisses. The
guests dispersed, and Germaine, refusing Constant's
entreaties that she remain in his room, returned to her
boudoir; there she washed her arms with eau de cologne
and remarked to her maid that Constant would inspire in
her "insurmountable physical revulsion."[85]

Constant's pioneering of the "Coppet dose of opium,"[86] a phrase later coined by the mid-nineteenth-cen-
tury critic Sainte-Beuve to describe the histrionics of Germaine's milieu, henceforth became a form of emotional
blackmail frequently used by the hostess and her guests.
The precise date at which Germaine overcame her repug-
nance for Constant and stopped dousing herself with cologne when he touched her is not clear. Whenever their
liaison was first consummated, their literary partnership
was already official in 1795, when Germaine kissed her
father and her children good-bye and rode off with Constant to reconquer Paris. From that time on, they were
alternately in each other's arms or at each other's throats,
and he was the only man who was ever allowed to address
her as "Minette," as her father had.

The Directory has been as maligned as any period of
French history for its debauchery, economic chaos, and
corruption (there are parallels with postcommunist
Russia). When the most powerful and dissolute of the
five directors, Vicomte Paul de Barras, engineered
the overthrow of Robespierre in 1794, a new set of

unscrupulous entrepreneurs came to power. A tall, flamboyant bon vivant with a mane of wavy black hair, this former Jacobin aristocrat, who had been a popular member of Germaine's pre-Revolution salon, had recently built up a vast fortune through the bribes offered him by army contractors. He was also famous for quickly wearying of his mistresses and excelled at arranging good matches for them—one former paramour, Joséphine de Beauharnais, had been passed on to the promising young general Napoleon Bonaparte. In his leisure time, Barras lived like an Oriental potentate in his country mansion an hour from Paris, where he entertained requests for amnesty on the part of other prominent émigrés. Pressured by Mme de Staël, for instance, to obtain a high government post for her former lover, Talleyrand, after his return from the United States, Barras eventually appointed him foreign minister.

Under Barras's tutelage, and also as a reaction against Robespierre's puritanism, the Directory, which was inaugurated in the summer of 1795, was one of the century's most hedonistic eras. In the 1794–1795 season alone, 644 new public dance halls had been opened. The extravagant attire of Paris's *merveilleuses* and *incroyables*, euphemisms for the fastidiously attired fashion icons of each gender, were meticulously described in the daily press. The sans-culottes' familiar *tu* was quickly dropped to restore the formal *vous*. Opulent new dishes such as lobster thermidor were added to the culinary vocabulary. At the luxurious salons where the mode of antique dress was launched, it was chic to proclaim

Royalist sympathies and boast of one's arduous jail term under the Terror. Bordellos never did better business. As a token of national unity, Place de la Révolution, where thousands of aristocrats, Louis XVI himself, and, later, Robespierre, were guillotined, was renamed Place de la Concorde. "Balls and spectacles have replaced prisons and revolutionary committees," wrote Talleyrand upon returning from two years of exile in the United States. "Swarms of light-headed young men...dance...and sigh after the monarchy as they savor ices or yawn before fireworks."[87]

And yet the apparent gaiety of the Directory, dominated as it was by a new class of crassly materialistic profiteers, masked great popular despair. The harvests of 1794 and 1795 had been disastrous; the winters that followed were the harshest in years. Beggars swarmed in the streets. Queues at bakeries formed at 1 a.m. The suicide rate was unprecedented. Countless families died of cold. The Marquis de Sade, whose main source of revenue, his lands, had been confiscated by the Directory, noted that he was obliged to put his ink on top of a double-boiler to keep it from freezing. On May 20, 1795 (Prairial, as the massacre came to be called according to the revolutionary nomenclature for the months of the year), an immense crowd of hungry citizens gathered in front of the National Assembly to shout demands for bread and was charged by hordes of bayonet-wielding soldiers. Over ten thousand arrests were made, and hundreds killed.

Germaine and Benjamin Constant arrived in Paris five days after the Prairial tragedy. She moved into the Swedish Embassy on the rue du Bac. Constant took lodgings nearby. They were determined, for the time being, to back the Directory government. As corrupt as they were, Barras, Tallien, and several other colleagues had been Germaine's friends before the Revolution; she direly needed them to lobby for the return of those dear to her who had been exiled by the Jacobins. In the pamphlet she had coauthored with Constan tjust before returning to Paris, all citizens were called to rally to the defense of the Republic, whatever its weaknesses and failings, and to combat the rising tide of pro-Royalist sentiment that had begun to sweep France in 1795.

Moving back into the Swedish embassy, Germaine obviously had to reconcile with her husband, if only to maintain the privileges of her rank as an ambassadress. And they seldom seemed to have been on better terms. She reopened her salon in the rue du Bac with great panache, and before long it became a meeting place for the leading politicians of the time. Soon after returning to Paris she was steeped in politics. Through one powerful member of her milieu, Marie-Joseph Chénier, brother of the poet André Chenier, she successfully lobbied for the return of most of her exiled friends. But her passion for rescuing those of her own milieu did not extend to the masses of French citizens made hungry or homeless by the indifference of the Directory's rulers.

In few of Germaine's writings is her disinterest in the masses more obvious than in an essay on which she had collaborated with Constant, *"Réflexions sur la paix intérieure,"* which she withheld from large-scale distribution on the advice of friends. Offer civil rights to all classes, its message goes, but leave government in the hands of the well-heeled. The biographer J. Christopher Herold calls this text "a hymn to the sanctity of property and to the political rights of the propertied." The new constitution, which emerged in the summer of 1795, must have well pleased Germaine. It provided for a five-man Directory, a bicameral legislature, and voting rights limited to the wealthy. There had been an urgent need for a sturdy constitution, because tensions between Republicans and Royalists were becoming acute. On the morning of September 27, 1795 (13 Vendémiaire in revolutionary lingo), Royalist forces rose to arms and were ruthlessly put down by the promising young general to whom Barras had recently passed on a mistress: Napoleon Bonaparte.

Although Germaine totally approved of Bonaparte's reprisal, her close ties to several Royalists led some members of the government to suspect that she had backed the Royalist conspiracy—so suspect was she, in fact, that the Committee of Public Safety ordered her to leave France within ten days. For a few months she tried to live in Normandy, but any site she occupied immediately took on a paramilitary aspect, with a constant *va-et-vient* of friends and messengers; and at the end of the year the government reaffirmed more forcefully than ever its orders that she return to Switzerland. She arrived in Coppet, Benjamin in tow, on New Year's Day of 1796.

Having suffered a political setback, Germaine devoted herself again to the pursuit of romance. Her relationship with Constant doesn't seem to have yet become a romantic liaison; the object of her affection now was François de Pange, a young aristocrat who combined great courage and intelligence with a delicate physique (he would die within two years of tuberculosis). "A happy and cautious youth," Chénier had once characterized him, "gentle, amiable, and tranquil even in his loves"; Pange was in love with a cousin of his, whom he married in January 1796. Subsequent letters clearly state Germaine's disappointment about her failure to seduce Pange: "I have seen all my past life smashed into pieces, and now at the age of twenty-seven. . . . Whatever choice I make is painful: to regret all my past feelings and to work at my destiny makes me feel the lassitude of labor and the torment of passion."[88] To Pange, another time: "You are the only man who has made me understand that it was possible to love without expecting as much in return." In the early months of 1796, as she began a full year's exile in what she called "the magnificent horror" of Switzerland, Germaine's letters to Pange, with whom she remained good friends, express the restlessness that always seized her when she was forced to return to Coppet. "The universe is France, outside it, there is nothing,"[89] she wrote him. The French minister of police, called Cochon, reasserted his threat to arrest her if she set foot on French soil and even took care to plant a spy in her household, an agent posing as her valet who read all the letters she entrusted him to mail. Neither was she popular with her compatriots. The letters of Rosalie de Constant, Benjamin's cousin, a resident of Lausanne who enjoyed reporting on the activities of the "trop célèbre," as she called Germaine, exemplify Swiss citizens' negative feelings toward Necker's daughter. (These letters make it clear that by mid-1796 Germaine had finally acceded to Constant's advances, and they had become lovers. The extremely close intellectual comradeship that had always marked their relations makes this conjecture almost irrelevant.)

"The all too celebrated arrived at the party with her whole barnyard . . . she talks of nothing but Benjamin; she seems very much preoccupied with him. . . . " Two months later, describing another evening: "[Benjamin] was tugging at her neck and calling her his good little kitten . . . this tableau disgusted me a little, as did their jokes about the ambassador [Staël]." Two months later still: "She speaks of him [Benjamin] without the least reticence—'The man whom I love most in the world, the man whom I desire with all the life that is left me'— without realizing the scandal she creates."[90]

During her 1796 exile, Germaine heard disturbing reports about her estranged husband: it seems that M. de Staël was struggling for his job. The new young king of Sweden, the capricious Gustavus IV, had decided to marry a granddaughter of Russia's Catherine the Great. The project inevitably led to shifts in Swedish foreign policy. Relations with France took a backseat, and Staël was relieved of his post. After holding out for a few weeks at the embassy on the rue du Bac—since he was devoid of income, his home was besieged with creditors—he dropped in on his wife at Coppet to inform her of his dismissal. She decided that it was all the more essential for her to return to Paris to protect her fortune. As she was about to leave for the capital she sent Constant ahead with copies of her new book, *De l'Influence des passions sur le bonheur des individus et des nations.* Thanks to her many literary contacts, the work was swiftly published and much praised. The Directory government softened its sanctions on her and let her know that she could return to France as long as she remained at a distance of twenty miles from Paris. In the last week of the year Germaine traveled to Constant's country house at Hérivaux, a former abbey some twenty-five miles from the capital.

By the time Germaine arrived at Hérivaux, she was a few months pregnant with Constant's child. She spent most of her pregnancy there, not only for reasons of discretion, but also out of political caution. The elections of March 1797 gave the Royalists a majority in the Convention. Having been exiled two years earlier because of her associations with Royalists, Germaine, ever at odds with power, was now threatened with another eviction because of her association with Republicans. "The Republic exiled me," she wrote to a friend in Germany. "The Counterrevolution hangs me."[91]

Germaine returned to Paris to give birth to her child; her daughter, Albertine, was born in June in the Swedish Embassy on the rue du Bac. M. de Staël, Germaine wrote Mathieu de Montmorency, reacted to the event "with sympathy and solicitude."[92] Germaine had maintained one custom of the ancien régime: there were at least fifteen persons in her room when her child was born, and she seems to have conversed with them throughout most of the ordeal. This time around, she could perfectly well have claimed that the child was her husband's, for he had spent a few affectionate days with her at Coppet the previous September. But although she officially maintained that Albertine's father was M. de Staël, she always led Constant to believe that the girl was his child. Constant adored her, and Albertine's close resemblance to him—she even had his uniquely bright red hair—is evident proof.

Once the bothersome business of childbirth was over, Germaine swung into action again to save the Republic from another Royalist insurrection. She was a leader of the Constitutional Circle, or Club de Salm, founded by Constant to counteract the Royalist Club de Clichy. The allegiance was painful to her: the Club de Clichy contained many of her former friends. But the Republicans, though ignorant and unjust, could be influenced (so she rationalized it), whereas the Royalists could not. She accomplished another important political mission that year: she managed to obtain the Ministry of Foreign Affairs for her former lover Talleyrand. Two years earlier "the Bishop," as she called him, had been allowed to return from the United States, where he had been wretched. Back home in France, he was more penniless than ever, and Germaine badgered Barras into making him the minister of foreign affairs. Barras went further: he wisely fired his entire cabinet and appointed one that was more safely committed to the anti-Royalist Club de Salm. To protect the country from a counterrevolution, Barras also gave increasing power to the young man whose victories had made him the hero of western Europe, General Napoleon Bonaparte. In those years Germaine referred to Bonaparte as "the best republican in France, the most liberal of Frenchmen."[93]

Chapter 10

Napoleon Bonaparte

Napoleon Bonaparte first distinguished himself in 1793 when, as a twenty-four-year-old protégé of Robespierre, he won a decisive victory against the British in Toulon. Remembering the young brigadier general's extraordinary valor, it is to him that Barras turned two years later, when Royalists had staged their insurrection in September 1795 (Vendémiaire) in an effort to overturn the new constitution. Bonaparte's brisk and brutal putting down of Royalists (through "a whiff of grapeshot," as he called it) led Barras to promote him to commander-in-chief of the army of Italy. His next great triumphs were in Italy and in Austria: he had the pleasure of seeing Nice and Savoy annexed to France; shortly afterward he not only stopped Austrian forces' forays into French territory but also invaded the enemy's territory to a hundred miles from Vienna, forcing Austria to sue for peace.

On the domestic front, it was Bonaparte's splendidly trained army that made possible the coup d'état of August 1797 (Fructidor), which saved the nation from again being controlled by the Royalist majority in the Convention. The stratagem Bonaparte devised with Barras was the following: Deputies were summoned to an emergency session at the Tuileries, their habitual meeting place. Three hundred thousand troops dispatched by Napoleon surrounded the site. As Staël, an eyewitness, described it, "The grenadiers marched in square formations, as if the room were empty. The deputies, pushed against the wall, were forced to flee through the windows . . . still in their senatorial togas."[94] Overnight, 198 deputies whose convictions were not safely Republican were fired; Carnot and Barthélémy were expelled from the Directory; the press was placed under close censorship; and some 65 officials suspected of Royalist sympathies were deported to French Guiana. Rarely was an elected body toppled with such efficiency.

Germaine was accused by some of having had a hand in this plot, but although she may have been apprised of it beforehand she bore no responsibility for it. At considerable risk to herself, she had kept busy much of that summer quietly helping friends suspected of Royalist sympathies to escape. Moreover, no sooner had the August coup d'état occurred then she found herself at odds with the victors. Whereas more pragmatic and self-interested citizens shift with each change of regime and side with the party in power, it was in Germaine's rebellious nature to take the contrary course: as each new party came to power, she instinctually gravitated to the opposition. By the fall she was being attacked with equal vehemence by the Royalist press for having had a hand in the coup, and by the Republican press for having helped Royalists to escape it. Only the support of Barras—the scoundrel seemed capable of holding to a few loyal friendships—protected her from being prosecuted.

In December 1797 Bonaparte returned from Italy, having signed a victorious peace treaty at Campo Formio that further expanded France's control over that part of Europe. Talleyrand arranged a grand reception for him at the foreign ministry. Bonaparte's brief speech deeply impressed Germaine. She met him again four days later, at a more formal function held by the Directors at the Luxembourg Palace, and her enthusiasm for him grew apace. At that time, Bonaparte, just elected to the Institut de France, was posing as a man who desired above all to devote his life to scholarship and study. For the following year Germaine wooed him shamelessly, intimating that the greatest male mind in France should collaborate with the nation's greatest female spirit. Bonaparte's deeply misogynist (and typically Corsican) attitude toward women led him to panic at that possibility. As his taste in women shows—his ravishing, shallow wife Josephine is a perfect example—he gravitated exclusively to beautiful, submissive, feminine creatures and had an instinctual repulsion for powerful, intelligent ones. ("Madame, I do not like women to talk about politics," Staël quotes him as having told a spirited woman of Parisian society. "But in a nation where women's heads are cut off, sire," the lady answered, "it's natural that they'd want to know why"[95]). Aware of Germaine's bent for political machinations, and finding her physically repellent, Bonaparte was all the more determined to keep her at a safe distance.

These two brilliant citizens—Germaine de Staël and Napoleon Bonaparte—had a few things in common: their earnest Republicanism, their centrist political views, and their faith in the benefits of scientific progress. Both believed in the need to spread the liberal principles of the Revolution throughout Europe; both saw property as the foundation of the social order; both had a predilection for the immense, the melancholy, the infinite—like Germaine, Bonaparte passionately loved Ossian and Goethe's *Werther*. He even shared her life's central tenet—that enthusiasm was the source of all greatness. They both hated mockery: Germaine's witticisms at Bonaparte's expense were as painful to him as his verbal onslaughts were to her (he would call her "a shrew," "a crow," "a whore, and an ugly one at that,"[96] "a lower class knitting woman" [*une tricoteuse de bas étage*][97]).

But there the resemblances ended. Unlike Germaine, Bonaparte did not believe in the sovereignty of the people, or in the popular will, or in parliamentary debate. Whereas Germaine had a heartfelt, disinterested love for humanity, he despised the masses, had no use for anyone who was not clearly useful to him, and had no true friends. ("His force consists of an imperturbable egoism which neither pity, or attraction, or religion, or morality can in the least bit influence," Staël would write about him. "It could be said of him that he is the world's great bachelor."[98]) Whereas Germaine's gaffes and misjudgments came from her impulsiveness, her guilelessness, and her optimistic view of human nature, Bonaparte prided himself on always suspecting the worst in men, on basing all his decisions on cold calculation, and on being a master of deception. One biographer hit it on the mark when he wrote of Bonaparte that "in no man had so much grandeur been combined with so much cynicism."[99] Toqueville put it equally well: Bonaparte was as great as a man can be who "lacks the least shred of virtue."[100]

But it may be Germaine herself who eventually coined the most crushing descriptions of him:

> When in society he tried to give himself in turn an air of familiarity or of dignity, but he lacked the true tone of either, for he could only be natural in his despotism.[101] . . . An imperturbable face, a brazen silence, an insolence well combined with an imposing politeness, all that was well calculated to subdue.[102] . . . He knows how to make both good men and bad men uneasy, and the stifling air he weighs upon all that surrounds him has been a major cause of the ascendance he has had upon the French.[103] . . . There is something both hypocritical and falsely mild about him which resembles the velvet paw of a tiger.[104] . . . The conscience of a Wellington was 100 times worthier for the glory and prosperity of France than that of the infernal genius who found in men's baseness the vital center which Archimedes sought to lift up the world.[105]

Despite the disdain Bonaparte displayed toward Germaine in their early meetings, she initially maintained the delusion that she must serve as his advisor. Aware of that goal, the young general responded to her with increasing coarseness and viciousness. In an anecdote that typifies the early stage of their relationship, Germaine is sitting next to Bonaparte at a dinner given at Talleyrand's house. "Who is the greatest woman, alive or dead?" she asks the general. "The one, Madame, who has had the greatest number of children,"[106] the general replies and turns his back on her. For once, even Germaine was devoid of a clever retort. Upon such exchanges Germaine's appreciation of Bonaparte began to wane ("The only species of human creatures he did not understand well were those who were sincerely attached to some opinion,"[107] she later wrote of him. "When he encounters true honesty somewhere, his artifices seem disconcerted, as are a demon's machinations by the sign of the cross."[108])

But her resistance to him began in earnest in 1798, when he set out to effect the armed "liberation" of Switzerland—he needed the gold of Bern to defray the expenses of his Egyptian venture. Germaine was terrified for her father, whose financial survival depended on the Swiss status quo being maintained. She sent yet more letters to Bonaparte, pleading to no avail that the country be left in peace, emphasizing "the peace [this country] had enjoyed for several centuries."[109] She then hurried to Coppet to be at her father's side when the French troops arrived—she later commented that it was the first time she prayed for a French defeat. The invasion was over quickly and pacifically: Switzerland was reorganized under French occupation as the Helvetic Republic; Geneva was annexed to France; the gold of Berne was carried off to Paris to outfit the army of the Orient; and to Germaine's relief, the French troops treated her father with gentle respect.

Her reconciliation with the French was only temporary. Upon Bonaparte's orders, all her repeated forays into that country were systematically frustrated. She spent the years 1798 and 1799 at a dizzyingly nomadic pace, frantically trying to find a place from which she might not be evicted. She was at her father's estate, Saint-Ouen, for the summer of 1798 but was warned by the police that she must abide by Bonaparte's orders barring her from France, so she returned to Coppet. In January 1799 she took an apartment in Geneva, now in French territory, received another police warning, and dejectedly came home to her family domain. Hoping that her growing literary reputation might mollify the general, in April '99 she joined Constant in France and was once more expelled two months later. ("Far from being kind to those who distinguished themselves in some way, [Bonaparte] wished to turn all of those who had risen into a pedestal for his statue."[110]) She made yet another foray to Paris in the evening of November 9 (Brumaine 18), having heard that Bonaparte was about to stage his most radical coup d'état to date. The general's plans proceeded with characteristic swiftness: The members of the Directory were forced to resign, all of the legislative councils were dispersed, and a new government—the Consulate—was established. The three consuls were Bonaparte and two of the former directors, Sieyès and Pierre-Roger Ducos. But it was Bonaparte, soon to make himself First Consul, who was now clearly the master of France.

How did Constant fare in "this miserable gypsy life,"[111] as M. Necker referred to the nomadism imposed upon his daughter by Bonaparte? He hated it. While deeply, neurotically bound to Germaine, Constant all too frequently longed to be released from their relationship. As early as his daughter's birth in 1797, he had asked his aunt to find him a wife. "I must give happiness to somebody," he wrote her, "I need [a wife] to be happy."[112] He had learned early on that he could not give Germaine happiness because she was incapable of it; his desultory attempts to break loose from her would last another thirteen years.

And where was M. de Staël throughout this nomadic period of his wife's life? He was disintegrating in both body and mind. Having lost his ambassadorial post, he had no source of revenue, was still paying Mlle Clairona considerable annual pension, and was making huge dents in his wife's capital. Talleyrand, now foreign minister, intimated to the Swedish government that M. de Staël's reinstatement as ambassador would be well received by the French government. Young Gustavus IV, as neurotically capricious a monarch as any in Europe, partially acceded to Talleyrand's suggestion and made Staël minister plenipotentiary. M. de Staël enjoyed his post very briefly. Three months later Gustavus IV changed his mind again and broke off relations with France, giving poor Staël his final dismissal. For a year or so the former ambassador disappeared from view. In 1800 M. Necker received a letter from a Parisian citizen, who identified himself as a friend of Staël's, and was notifying all concerned that Staël was living in a small flat near the Concorde, destitute, sick, and uncared for. The news even reached Bonaparte, who pretended to take pity on him—it was yet one more way he could criticize Staël's wife. "Monsieur de Staël is in the most abject misery, and his wife gives dinners and balls," he wrote his brother Joseph. "Have we reached an age in which we may trample underfoot not only morality, but even duties more sacred than those that unite mothers and children, without incurring the blame of decent people?"[113] Necker, terrified that his son-in-law's debts might have a disastrous effect on his own fortune, eventually drew up a formal agreement whereby Staël would be paid a small annual allowance. The modesty of this pension, however, forced him to stop making payments to Mlle Clairon. She eventually sued him; police came to his flat at the Concorde to cart away all his belongings, and the commotion led him to have a stroke.

Reenter Germaine, who had been officially separated from Staël since 1798. In the spring of 1802, alarmed by reports about her former husband's condition, she went to his flat and found a half-senile paralytic. She carted him off toward Coppet, but Staël did not even make it to the Swiss frontier. In the town of Poligny, before the border, his symptoms took a turn for the worse. Germaine stayed at his bedside for the remaining two days. He died on the night of May 8, and Germaine's carriage rode into Coppet followed by a hearse.

Responding to one particular letter of condolence, Germaine set down her feelings with perfect honesty:

"I was looking forward joyfully to making up, through my care, for the sentiments I had been unable to give him. . . . I am very much affected by this death, and I shall never find any consolation for my inability to make him happy. . . when he abandoned himself to me."[114] In sum, her conscience needled her, and she felt guilt—a guilt not totally justified, since Staël had been digging his own grave all along through his sloth, his ineptitude, his addiction to gambling, and his foolish liaison.

The reader may remember that a condition for M. de Staël's marriage to Mademoiselle Necker, some fifteen years earlier, was that France sell part of the island of St. Barthélémy to Sweden. That area of the island would be sold back to France over half a century after Staël's death, in 1877, for the equivalent of 50,000 dollars.

Chapter 11

"I Shall Break Her, I Shall Crush Her"

For the next fourteen years, until Bonaparte's fall in 1814, Germaine de Staël's motto for her struggle against the French leader might well have been inspired by Voltaire's slogan, *"Résistez l'infâme!"* Though she would have been loath to admit it, it was Bonaparte's relentless persecution of her and her uncompromising resistance to him, quite as much as her writings, that made her into an illustrious and hugely influential cosmopolitan figure. The tyrant was, in sum, the whetstone for her literary genius.

Staël's principal works, in this reader's view, were *De la littérature* (1800), *Delphine* (1802), *Corinne* (1807), *De l'Allemagne* (1810), *Dix années d'exil* (1812), and *Considérations sur la Révolution francaise* (1819.) Here are some of the principal ideas—many of them loathsome to Bonaparte—expressed in these works.

The most frequent target of Staël's derision:
The smug, self-centered provincialism of the French. Her own origins—Swiss and Protestant—as well as her extensive knowledge of British and German literature, saved her from the parochialism of her adopted country. One reason she so enraged Bonaparte is that she held

other nations' cultures, especially England's and Germany's, in such high esteem: the German nation, for instance, "works for the amelioration of mankind better than we do; it perfects the Enlightenment";[115] it is also "the nation best suited to the development of philosophical thought."[116] The following statements must also have made Bonaparte wince: "The advantages given to women, in England, are the principal cause of the fecundity of British literature . . . tyrannical laws, vulgar desires, corrupt principles, have ruled women's destinies, whether in ancient times, or in Asia, or in France."[117] "We owe most French novels we love to our imitation of British models."[118] "In recent years, the situation in France has been contrary to the enhancement of talent and of the human spirit than it has been in most periods of history."[119] Adamant about proclaiming France's superiority in every area of human endeavor, vehemently resenting Staël's intimations that other cultures were superior to France's, Bonaparte banned her writings for being "un-French."

Staël on the French Revolution

This was one of her most incisive contributions to French political thought: she bitterly condemned the Terror and the death of the royal couple but she never deplored the Revolution itself. Ideals, she emphasized, could not be abolished every time a crime was committed in their name. The French Revolution, in fact, was "The triumph of the Enlightenment," the only way to eventually achieve "the establishment of a representative government towards which the human spirit everywhere aspires."[120] But she remained deeply puzzled by the fact that human beings in the age of the Enlightenment could have acted with such bestiality during the Terror. She ardently rejected the notion, widely held among Royalists, that the Revolution's crimes were traceable to the Republican system. She believed, instead, that they were traceable to the corruption wrought upon a nation through "the abuses of the Ancien Régime," by the depravity casued by its "absolute want of public morality," by the principle of inequality upon which it was founded and by the class hatreds it incited.[121] She also emphasized that the Republic arrived in France before the Enlightenment had time to prepare the nation for it. "The Republic was founded fifty years before the citizens's spirits were ready for it," she writes in *Des circonstances actuelles de la Révolution,* "the masses had recourse to the Terror to establish it."[122] In a sly dig at Bonaparte, Staël also underscored that philosophers, rather than military men, had created the Revolution, and that philosophers must continue to direct its course. "Generals," she wrote, "solely considered for their military prowess, will have far less influence on the condition of France than thinkers speaking their thoughts in the Assembly or in their books." Neither would Bonaparte have been thrilled by the following passage: "The traits mutual to the French and the British revolutions are the following: A king led to the scaffold by the spirit of democracy, a military leader grasping power and restoring the former dynastic principles."[123]

Staël on women:

She was the first writer of either gender to point out that the Revolution of 1789, which should have brought women greater liberty and equality, paradoxically lowered their standing in French society. "Since the Revolution," she wrote, "men have thought that it was politically and morally useful to reduce women to the most absurd mediocrity."[124] Staël was also the first French writer to emphasize the general injustices plaguing women, and the first to note that society makes it impossible for them to reconcile personal achievement or notoriety with romantic love. Staël praised women ardently; she sees them as having played a role, in the history of the West, as beneficial and civilizing as the Christian faith. She warned women, however, to not proclaim their equality with men, to not try competing with them in those activities that so far have been their domain. ("In monarchies [women] have ridicule to fear, and in republics, hatred."[125]) On the contrary, she urged women to nurture those qualities inherent in their gender, which is "endowed with the greater sensibility."[126] They must hide, if not sacrifice, their talents from the eyes of the men they love (an advice she hardly followed herself). She particularly deplored the plight of gifted, superior women, who inevitably find frustration and dejection in their romantic lives. She seems to have traced some sources of her own personal unhappiness to her own unique gifts. "One must constantly try to have a new success since one is still hated for past successes.... Unhappy life, thrice unhappy life!"[127] And she saw women's continuing enlightenment as vital to the progress of mankind. "It is essential to the happiness of society for women to develop their spirit and their rational powers.. . . Enlightening, instructing, perfecting women as fully as men . . . is still the best path for all social and political goals to which one wishes to assure lasting foundations."[128] If a woman seeks glory for herself, Staël warns, she will only find *"un deuil éclatant du bonheur,"*[129] a wonderfully cryptic phrase that one might best translate as "a bliss bursting forth with mourning."

To contemporary readers, Staël will seem at her most old-fashioned when she writes that women should aspire to be associated with great men and be content to share the glory men find in political or social actions. And many of us will snarl at her warning that women will always be in need of a man's support, his protection, his love. Notwithstanding these handicaps Staël emphasizes women's superior gifts for understanding, giving, and describing love and notes that their "mobile and delicate"[130] sensibility was central to the development of the novel form. Few of these ideas could have delighted Bonaparte. But the two notions of Staël's that most enraged him (at the time she propounded them he was about to sign the Concordat with the Pope, a decree that restored to the clergy all privileges they had enjoyed before the Revolution) had to do with divorce and Protestantism: Any unreturned love justifies divorce, if not suicide, Staël writes, for a woman's ideal resides in mutual conjugal love. As for Protestantism—her religion—she saw it as superior to Roman Catholicism because it was less likely to become an instrument of temporal power; and she seems to have looked on the Reformation as one of those historical epochs that, like most revolutions, "most efficaciously worked for the perfectibility of the human race."[131]

Staël on enthusiasm:
Her faith in the importance of enthusiasm brought the word back to its ancient roots: its Greek origins (en + theos) denote "having God in us." Without enthusiasm, she believed, human goodness cannot be realized. "Enthusiasm is to conscience," as she put it, "what honor is to duty."[132] Reason and virtue are guides to existence, but the fire of enthusiasm is their very life: it inspires in us the love of beauty, and the pleasure we take in dutifulness; it underlies all genuine sensibility and oversees the development of all generous ideas. "Those philosophers who're inspired by enthusiasm are those whose work shows the greatest exactitude and patience."[133] "Only enthusiasm can counterbalance our tendency to selfishness, and it is this divine sign that makes us into immortal creatures."[134] Enthusiasm is also the ultimate defense against frivolity, and the most lasting of passions: "If enthusiasm does not defend our heart and spirit, they are overtaken by that denigration of beauty which blends insolence and gaiety."[135] "The storm of passions passes, the pleasures of self-love wane, only enthusiasm is never altered."[136] One could fill a nice pamphlet with Staël's quotes on this sentiment: "Enthusiasm is the emotion that offers us the greatest happiness, the only one that offers it to us, the only one

able to sustain human destiny in whatever situation destiny places us."[137] "Enthusiasm is tolerant," she also wrote, "not out of indifference, but because it leads us to recognize the value and beauty of things."[138] "Is the human soul indifferent to the beauties of great tragedies, to the divine sounds of celestial music, to the enthusiastic strains of martial music?" she asked. "Why would it refuse itself eloquence? The human soul needs exaltation."[139] "What is man if he does not always reach for the highest ideals and sentiments? All destinies need a luminous future for which the soul reaches. Warriors need their glory, thinkers need liberty, sensitive men need God. One must not stifle those moments of enthusiasm . . . there is morality in all sources of enthusiasm."[140]

Staël's "De la littérature":

Violently attacked in the Bonapartist press when it was published in 1800, it is a hugely influential book, the pioneering work of what we now call comparative literature. Throughout the century that followed Germaine's death, it remained an inspirational tract for left-of-center liberals confronted by the onslaught of reaction. An uneven text, it exemplifies the virtues and defects of works written by great conversationalists and improvisers: Staël's knowledge of any literature that did not pertain to France and Switzerland was shaky. One flinches at the facility with which she generalizes on subjects she knew next to nothing about, and at the ineptitude of many of her literary judgments (she looked on Ossian as the father of English literature and believed the Irish were a Germanic race). Yet *De la littérature*, a paean to the moral and spiritual benefits of novels and poetry, offers as exalted a view of literature as has ever been penned by any writer. She bestows upon it a parareligious power: "Poetry is a momentary possession of all that is sought by our soul. Writers' talent leads the barriers of existence to disappear and to transform mortals' vague hopes into brilliant images."[141] "One above all admires certain writings because they have uniquely moved all the moral powers of our being."[142]

Literature, in Staël's view, also has deeply political implications: By "refining and elevating" [143] citizens' character, it can augment the enlightenment necessary to democracy, and help to cure, or at least calm, the human tendency to violence; reading good literature might even lessen the crime rate throughout the world by developing in human beings the capacity to be moved. It encourages the emergence of national collective identity even when a nation does not yet exist, as in the case of Italy or Germany in her time. And it is an essential feature of moral or spiritual regeneration in an era when "the perfectibility of the human species has become an object of mocking derision on the part of those who believe intellectual occupations to be a form of imbecility, and only hold in regard those faculties that have instantaneous results."[144] (Such sly digs at Bonaparte abound in Staël's writings.) Finally, literature creates in citizens an intellectual cosmopolitanism that can greatly enhance a nation's sense of freedom; this notion would also be odious to Bonaparte, who believed in exclusively nationalist fervor.

Germaine's capacity for self-delusion and, even more strikingly, her frequent naïveté were truly amazing for a person of her intelligence: she had actually expected that the huge success enjoyed by *De la littérature* might improve her standing vis-à-vis Bonaparte. She was extremely slow to realize the depth of the abyss that separated her from the First Consul. No sooner had *De la Littérature* been published than the government press went on the attack. The "Journal des Débats" made particularly clear Bonaparte's displeasure with Germaine's criticisms of French culture, which must have been merely reported to him, for his antipathy was hardly based on extensive reading. He openly admitted to his brother Lucien that he had studied the book "for at least a quarter of an hour" and could not understand it. "In spite of concentrating all my faculties," he told Lucien, "I failed to discover a meaning in any of those ideas that are supposed to be so profound. The devil take me if I could make any sense of it."[145]

Why did Bonaparte not persecute Germaine even more brutally than he did, seeing the antipathy she expressed to him in her writings from 1800 on? It is because he was greatly beholden to certain individuals and ideological groups within which Germaine, the champion networker, had powerful friends and protectors. They included his own two brothers, most of his marshals, his foreign minister Talleyrand, influential bankers and industrialists who sought benefit in remaining friends with her. Also in Germaine's sway were Bonaparte's brother-in-law,

Joachim Murat, and his two principal military leaders, Generals Junot and Bernadotte.

Above all there was Bonaparte's police minister, her great friend Joseph Fouché: ex-monk, ex-Jacobin, he was one of the most fascinating and mysterious men of his generation, and Germaine herself would admit that "there was no discernible morality in his conduct . . . he often spoke of virtue as if it were an old wives' tale."[146] This survival artist who successfully switched sides with every change of government from the Bourbons to Robespierre to Napoleon, and continued to retain immense authority under the reign of Louis XVIII—a forty-year span of power-wielding—has been regarded as the organizer of the first modern police state. He loved intrigue and power, but he above all loathed miscalculation, which he had begun to see evidence of in Bonaparte's demeanor. His distaste for doing any evil beyond that which was strictly necessary led to the riposte for which he is most famous: In 1803, criticizing Napoleon's execution of Louis XVI's cousin, the Duc d'Enghien, Fouché exclaimed, "It's worse than a crime, Sire; it's a blunder!"[147] Whether out of admiration for Germaine's stature, or out of a sense that she would ultimately be useful to him, he seemed to have thought it would be a blunder to not remain unfailingly loyal to her.

As for Germaine's view of the vastly increased power that the events of Brumaire offered Bonaparte, she had been in favor of it because she still looked on him as a lesser evil. A Jacobin or a Royalist regime would have ended all hopes for centrist citizens of her ilk, she rationalized, whereas Bonaparte's autocratic tendencies could be restrained by those who had enabled his ascent to power. She kept chafing at Bonaparte's increasing opposition to her holding a salon, which she referred to as "a hospital for defeated parties."[148] Her drawing room, she protested, was not a rallying point for anti-Bonapartists, but a sounding board for public opinion. Why should the "man of the hour," as the First Consul was called by many of his fans, fear a powerless woman who merely facilitated intelligent discussions in her drawing room? Her protestations missed the point. She failed to see the principal reason for Bonaparte's dread of her: It was not that she was entertaining opposition parties in her salon; it was that the very clique that had helped him rise to power supported her. After every attempt to silence Germaine, the First Consul was besieged by blood relatives and highly placed associates who begged him to be clement toward her; such meddling greatly increase the anxiety she caused him, and his aversion to her eventually became one of his central obsessions.

It should be noted, moreover, that Bonaparte was never satisfied to have anyone remain politely silent about him. "Tell the newspaper editors," he wrote to Fouché, "that I shall hold them responsible not for their criticism, but for their failure to praise."[149] Hypocritical praise, to the Corsican's eyes, was preferable to candid criticism, or even silence, particularly in Paris. As for outright detraction, he did not yet care what Germaine said about him in Vienna, London, or Milan, but he dreaded the possibility that when in Paris she could incite his supporters to disparage him. If Germaine had grasped the depth of Bonaparte's rage against her she might have conducted herself with more discretion.

"Why does Mme de Staël not rally to my government?" the First Consul once asked his brother Joseph. "What does Mme de Staël want? The right to stay in Paris? I'll grant it to her. What does she want?" "Good lord," said Germaine when Bonaparte's query was reported to her, "it's not a question of what I want, but of what I think."[150] However often she had promised to stay out of politics, to remain silent, she was congenitally incapable of refraining herself, at any time of day or night, from saying what she thought.

Here is a typical example of how Bonaparte's opposition could deeply affect Germaine's life: Under the Consulate, the constitution provided for a bicameral system consisting of a Tribunate, whose members discussed government-proposed laws without voting on them, and a legislative assembly that voted on the same laws without discussing them. Benjamin Constant, who claimed dual Swiss and French citizenship, presented himself as a candidate for the Tribunate. Germaine asked Sieyès to support Constant's candidacy, and Constant got his wish. The Tribunate held its first session on January 1, 1800; and on January 5 Constant was to make his maiden speech, one in which he planned to criticize a government-proposed law which he considered to be a threat to the independence of the Tribunate. His speech had been drafted under Germaine's supervision, and at a dinner on the eve of his presentation he was warned by a few friends that the First Consul would not take kindly to it. "If I speak my mind," Constant warned Germaine, "our drawing room will be deserted tomorrow."[151] However aware she was of her own "taste for society,"[152] Germaine begged him to speak his conscience, whatever the social consequences. And he did. Accusing the government of "rushing through proposals to us on the wing, in the hope that we shall be unable to catch them," he concluded that without an independent Tribunate, "there would be nothing left but servitude and silence, a silence that all Europe would hear."[153]

Germaine had planned a dinner in Constant's honor on the evening that followed his speech. By 5 p.m. she had received ten notes from guests excusing themselves, including one from Talleyrand, who owed her his job, if not his survival. Meanwhile, at the Tuileries, Bonaparte was displaying one of his bouts of "calculated rage." "The Tribunate has some twelve or fifteen metaphysicians who should be drowned," he thundered. "Those intellectuals are a vermin I carry in my clothes; I will shake them off."[154] The press, the following day, echoed the First Consul's anger, focusing it on Germaine; she was "an intriguer" who should immediately take "the road to Switzerland," a woman who "writes on morality, which she does not practice . . . and on the virtues of her sex, which she lacks."[155] Fouché then summoned Germaine to his Police Ministry and explained that the First Consul held her responsible for Constant's speech. She indignantly denied the charge. Go to the country for a few days, Fouché advised her, the First Consul might quiet down. This time, Fouché was wrong. Germaine returned to Paris a few weeks later and immediately understood that not only was she ostracized by Bonaparte, but by society at large. Arriving at a ball to which she'd been asked because the First Consul, though invited, was known to have refused, Germaine was greeted with silent stares. Any group she approached dispersed and faced the other way. She backed into a corner, where she sat alone until her loyal friend Delphine de Sabran, the widow of General de Custine, came to her rescue and sat by her side for the rest of the evening.

Bonaparte's prestige that season was enhanced by his difficult victory at Marengo—another battle that Germaine hoped the French would lose. On his way to Italy, as Bonaparte passed through Geneva, he allowed Necker, whom he referred to as "a dull, bloated pedant" to call on him and intercede for his daughter. Notwithstanding his poor impression of the savant of Coppet, Bonaparte promised he would allow Mme de Staël to reside in Paris, provided she was prudent. Wishing to wait for the fall season before returning to the capital, Germaine headed for Coppet, where she spent a quieter summer than usual getting reacquainted with her children. Auguste, the older of the two sons she'd had with Narbonne, was now ten; Albert was eight. She decided to tutor them herself that summer, an experience made erratic by constant interruptions—visitors, the dictation of urgent letters. Her oldest, Auguste, an eager and gifted student, took in all he could. Albert, a rather scatterbrained boy, remained apathetic. Both the boys' interests were in science and mathematics, for which Germaine cared little. Only in her daughter, Albertine, then three years old, would she eventually find the cultural sensibility and passions she expected in a child of hers.

This quiet summer in Coppet—her relationship with Constant was by then drained of most sexual passion—led Germaine to have many bitter reflections about the men in her past. "I live with a memory of men in my past the way others live with a physical ailment," she wrote. "The men I have loved the most are Narbonne, Talleyrand, and Mathieu [de Montmorency].... New friends have become dear to me, but it is the past which stirs my imagination...."[156] Why had romantic bliss eluded her, she wondered increasingly as she grew older. Why couldn't she find happiness with a man, as other women did?

To answer such questions would have taken an introspective candor Germaine was not capable of. If asked why Germaine's lovers had begun to tire of her after an average of six months, Constant, for one, would have given the following answers: She asked for a happiness that could only be found in serene domesticity but refused to sacrifice fame and ambition to achieve that state. Her hyperactive pace greatly slackened the work of any man who shared her life (it would take Constant, a very rapid writer, some ten years to finish his dissertation on world religions while living at Coppet). Moreover, she rescued men from obscurity only to make them objects of notoriety. "[I am] pursued by her incessant reproaches, always in the public view. . . and never holding the tiller of my own existence," Constant complained in his diary about his relationship with Germaine. Another time, even more condemningly: "I have never known a woman who was more continuously exacting. . . . Everybody's entire existence, every hour, every minute, for years on end, must be at her disposition, or else there is an explosion like all thunderstorms and earthquakes put together."[157]

What Constant could not phrase in psychological terms, the vocabulary not having been invented yet, was that Germaine clearly suffered from what we now call manic depression, or bipolar disorder. The ailment had already afflicted her in childhood, when she had a breakdown while suffering from her mother's brutal educational tactics. Symptoms of bipolar disorder continued to be evident throughout her life: her intense restlessness; her alternations of elation and despondency; her compulsion to converse into the dawn hours, her general hyperactivity and insomnia (as one of her colleagues at Juniper Hall had observed, "she sleeps only a few hours and spends the rest of her time in uninterrupted and furious activity"); her delusions of grandeur, well reflected in her long-held certainty that her books' success would move Bonaparte to be her friend; the occasional hallucinations that would plague her in later years; her frequent fits of hysteria, her predilection for melodramatic rhetoric and for creating violent scenes. Few men would have the patience or resilience to share their lives with a woman who combined these characteristic bipolar symptoms with a personality as forceful and dominating as Germaine's. And however vile Benjamin Constant's behavior might occasionally be, one cannot help being moved by the loyalty that led him to remain at her side throughout her "explosions . . . thunderstorms and earthquakes."

Thanks to Bonaparte's visit with M. Necker, during which he promised to temporarily lift the taboo forbidding Paris to her, Germaine spent the winter of 1800–1801 in the capital. She tirelessly attended receptions, operas, and balls, and also weekend parties at Joseph Bonaparte's estate in the Paris suburbs. At her own soirees "the lambs grazed with the wolves," as she put it. Austrian, Spanish, Russian, and Swedish ambassadors mingled with Bonaparte's siblings, ex-Jacobins rubbed elbows with Royalists and returned émigrés. It was during this season that Germaine met Bonaparte for the second time, at a formal reception. Having sought this opportunity for over a year, she did not want to waste it and, still hoping to charm him, had rehearsed a list of answers to respond to the questions she anticipated from him.

Alas, the First Consul's questions turned out to be unexpectedly coarse, far coarser than she could ever have imagined them to be. As he passed through the throng with his brother Lucien at his side, he stopped before her and pretended to scrutinize with interest her imposing decolletage. "No doubt," he said, "you have nursed your children yourself?" Germaine, for once, was left tongue-tied. "You see," the First Consul quipped to his brother, "she refuses to say yes or no."[158] Within a few months, she was in even greater disfavor with Bonaparte, once again due to Constant. Bonaparte, shaken by a murder attempt he escaped while driving to the opera, had 130 Jacobins deported without due process. Constant instantly spoke out at the Tribunate against such arbitrary procedure. This time Bonaparte silenced his critics by suppressing several newspapers and exiling a few more Jacobins. He also sent warnings to Mme de Staël that for her own good, she should stop inciting Constant. She left Paris to spend the summer in Coppet. Upon returning to Paris in November, she found her troubles with Bonaparte had multiplied, again due to Constant's accusatory speeches against the government. Bonaparte expelled Constant and nineteen other members of the Tribunate and asked Fouché to widen his network of spies, and to inform him in "the greatest detail" of any dissent.

From then on everything that was said in the salons of the Faubourg St. Honoré, particularly in Germaine's, reached Bonaparte's ears. Mme de Genlis, a literary lady of mediocre talents who had always envied and hated Germaine for her success, acted as Bonaparte's special agent in the Faubourg. When informed by Genlis that Germaine had referred to the First Consul as an "ideophobe," (she had been alluding to his sarcastic remarks concerning "ideologues"), he called in both his brothers to complain. "I can smell Mme de Staël from a mile away," he said, seated in the bathtub. "A fine thing!... Ideophobe! Why not hydrophobe?" He hit the bathwater with his fist, splashing brother Joseph from head to foot. "Advise her not to block my path," he added. "Or else I shall break her, I shall crush her. Let her keep quiet, it's the wisest course she can take."[159] Yet such crises left him all the more irritated at Germaine because he could not accuse her of any specific misdeed, and his inability to prove her guilt merely increased his paranoid hatred of her.

On May 8, 1802, the day M. de Staël died at a roadside inn, Bonaparte's consular term was extended for ten years; three months later, a plebiscite made him Consul for life, a dress rehearsal for the emperorship he would bestow on himself two years later. That very season a new book by M. Necker reached the public, his *Last Views on Politics and Finance,* in which the seer of Coppet did his daughter an enormous disservice by once more criticizing Bonaparte. He expressed displeasure at the new constitution and warned against the danger of an overly powerful military dictatorship. Bonaparte, as usual, was sure that Germaine had incited her father and swore again that she would never be allowed to set foot anywhere in France except Geneva, which had been occupied by the French for the past few years. "I shall defy his fury," Germaine wrote to a friend upon hearing of Bonaparte's threat. "He fears me," she told another. "This is what makes my joy and pride and terrifies me at the same time." "What matters in the nature of character is not whether one holds this or that opinion," she wrote to still another correspondent. "What matters is how proudly one upholds it." When her first published novel, *Delphine,* was issued in December 1802, she inserted a fairly obvious insult to Bonaparte in its preface. She was not concerned with officials' reaction to her book, she said, but with that of the public, which was "a silent but enlightened France."[160]

The novel takes place from 1790 to 1792, the critical period of Germaine's romance with Narbonne. Delphine, a kind, passionate, yet chaste woman, and a dazzling conversationalist (Germaine always injected some of her own characteristics into her heroines), welcomes the Revolution, seeing it as a historical necessity. The aristocratic milieu she moves in, however, is hostile to the Revolution and brings about her demise. She has fallen in love with Léonce de Mondoville, whose character is flawed by his susceptibility to public opinion (the similarity to Narbonne is obvious). A weak-willed, irresolute man, instead of following his inner convictions of Delphine's purity he believes rumors that accuse her of immoral behavior and is persuaded to marry a woman he does not love. The villain of the story is Léonce's mother-in-law, the charming but devious and greedy Mme de Vernon, who is closely modeled on Talleyrand ("I hear that in her novel Mme de Staël has disguised both herself and me as women,"[161] Talleyrand quipped upon reading the book). Mme de Vernon confirms Léonce's suspicions about Delphine to snap him up for her own daughter. Delphine ultimately retires to a Swiss convent, where a venal abbess, Léonce's aunt, forces her to take vows.

Upon finally hearing the truth about Delphine's virtue, Léonce, whose wife has expediently died, gallops off to Delphine's convent and convinces her to renounce her monastic vows. Delphine agrees, but the following day she learns that Léonce has chosen the political path opposite to hers: he has joined the émigré army. As Delphine hurries to his side in hopes of dissuading him from enlisting with Royalist forces she learns that the émigré army took him prisoner before he had a chance to join them, and that he is about to be executed as a traitor. Realizing that she has failed to save his life, Delphine takes poison and dies as she watches Léonce being shot to death. This great bad novel is a blistering attack against loveless marriage and religious bigotry, a paean to the superiority of British society over France's, and a polemic for women's rights.

Reading *Delphine* was like watching a parade of Bonaparte's bêtes noires, and even though he may merely have heard accounts of it, the First Consul was swift to strike back. Already infuriated by Necker's book, he reacted to *Delphine*'s publication with unprecedented spite. He even persuaded the elector of Saxony to forbid the sale of *Delphine* at the Leipzig Fair (the center of the European book trade). And of course he once more closed Paris to Germaine, threatening to have her "taken back to the border by gendarmes" if she ever set foot in the capital. She tried one last desperate tack: she prevailed on her father to lobby for her. Necker wrote a cringing letter to one of Bonaparte's chief aides, Consul Lebrun, begging him to be clement to Germaine, and apologizing for her "careless utterances." The answer, predictably, was negative. "The First Consul does not care to be thought so weak and imprudent as to allow his administration to become the butt of sarcasm,"[162]

Lebrun wrote back. Ever optimistic, still hoping that her oppressor would change his mind, totally uncertain as to where her future lay, Germaine was in an excruciating state of indecision. She had always tended to insomnia, and her sleeplessness now became acute. It is at this moment of her life, at the age of thirty-seven, that she began to take opium, on which she would become, over the years, increasingly, tragically dependent.

The habit of taking opium, which was derived from the unripe seeds of a species of poppy (Papaver somniferum) that grew abundantly in Great Britain's colonies in India, was not at all stigmatized in the early nineteenth century. Introduced into the European continent in the late eighteenth century, it was originally used for medicinal purposes, as a miracle cure for a wide variety of ailments: headaches, arthritis, children's colic, depression, insomnia, chest infections, diarrhea, dysentery, neuralgia, stomach pains of all sorts. Sold in the form of powders or pastes that could be diluted in water, wine, or brandy, opium was obtainable without prescriptions, for modest prices, in pharmacies and in a variety of other shops—grocers, tobacconists, even tailors and shoemakers. But as medical authorities started to realize in midcentury, when restrictions began to be imposed on its use, what had begun as an efficient painkiller often became, among intellectuals on both sides of the Channel, a recreational and very addictive drug.

Samuel Taylor Coleridge's, Thomas de Quincy's, and Charles Baudelaire's opium habits are the most documented addictions of nineteenth century literature.

It is less well-known that Charles Dickens' experiments
with opium, which he first took to allay a chronic cough,
are reflected in his dark novel *The Mystery of Edwin
Drood;* that Sir Walter Scott wrote his finest novel,
Bride of Lamermoor, and Hector Berlioz composed his
"Symphonie Fantastique," while under the influence
of opium; that Elizabeth Barrett Browning took it to
assuage her headaches and became a lifelong addict, as
did Bramwell Bronte, Emily's, Anne's, and Charlotte's
brother. One popular Victorian novelist, Wilkie Collins, a
lifelong addict, took great pride in his habit, proselytizing
for a substance that "stimulates the brain and steadies
the nerves."[163] Edgar Allan Poe, Théophile Gautier, the
painter Meissonier, the poets Gérard de Nerval, and
John Keats are among the numerous artists who sought
the alternations of serene somnolence and exaltation
experienced by opium users. Germaine de Staël's use of
the drug, however, was bound to affect her health all
the more nefariously because she was a manic depressive,
already plagued with alternations of elation and despair.
One is left saddened by the number of years stolen from
her life by the combined afflictions of bipolar disorder
and opium use.

Throughout the years that Germaine was suffering the
persecutions and the psychological distress inflicted by
Napoleon for publishing *Delphine,* Constant's state of
mind was as tormented as hers. And no torment was
greater than his ambivalent attitude toward his "Minette,"
as he called Germaine. His journal entries show that

notwithstanding the "great intellectual rapport" that still bound them, by 1802 he was out of love with her and suffering increasingly from her fits of manic temper. "Scene upon scene, torment upon torment,"[164] he confided to his journal about their life together. His passion could be briefly rekindled after one of her rare moments of selfless tenderness, and it was typical of his wavering character that he was equally incapable of loving and leaving her. Constant and Germaine both contributed to the torments of their "fatal liaison," as Constant referred to the relationship. He had a low opinion of himself, and Germaine's long accusatory orations against him, which could last until the dawn hours, greatly deepened his sense of inadequacy. They were both aware, however, that they brought out the best of each other's intellectual faculties, and if Germaine had more frequently expressed her affection, she might have maintained her spell over him more firmly. As their mutual friend, the scholar Jean-Charles Sismondi, recollected after their deaths: "No one has known Madame de Staël unless he has seen her with Benjamin Constant. . . . He alone has the power, through an intelligence equal to hers, to bring all her intellect into play . . . to kindle an eloquence, a depth of feeling and thought she would never reveal in all their brilliance except in his presence; neither was he ever truly himself except at Coppet."[165]

So each of the tortured, often quarreling, former lovers realized, with increasing bitterness, the depth of their dependence on each other. There had been talk of marriage, and curiously, it was Germaine who refused

Constant's repeated proposals. A considerable snob (especially when it came to titles), Germaine feared the loss of her social rank; she equally dreaded that her children's standing in society, and her daughter's chances of making a brilliant marriage, might be compromised by such a union. As for Constant, his utterly confused emotions about his relations to Germaine are made clear in the following passage of his journal: "It is a terrible relationship *a man who no longer loves* and a woman who does not want to stop being loved," he wrote. "The idea of losing me makes Germaine more anxious to keep me . . . and *since I really still love her,* the anguish that plagues her when she fails to find in me the feelings she needs causes me great pain."[166] (The italics are mine.)

Constrained by Bonaparte's orders, Constant and Germaine spent the winter of 1802–1803 in Geneva. In his journals, Constant complains that he is tired of being "swept away in her whirlwind";[167] that he is weary of sharing the criticism and scandals caused by Germaine's conduct; that he is exhausted by being kept up late every night by her social gatherings or her tantrums; that he is fed up with being kept from his studies and his writing by her hectic schedule. He was obsessed by the notion that, if only to get enough sleep, he must find a woman who could offer motherly understanding and a gentle, submissive sensuality. So while continuing to sate his lust by attending brothels ("the sanctuary of the timid,"[168] as a former biographer of Staël's has called such institutions), he tried having affairs. The closest he came to finding his ideal woman was one Mrs. Lindsay, née O'Dwyer, a former courtesan (and that at best) who was praised by Chateaubriand as possessing a noble soul and intellect. Burdened with two bastard children, at thirty-seven she was elegant, well-educated, and still beautiful.

Constant courted Mrs. Lindsay in his usual hysterical manner, "I love you like a madman,"[169] etc. She surrendered to him, he offered marriage, then Germaine stepped in. Proving again her powers of seduction, paying no more attention to Mrs. Lindsay than she would to a new guppy in a fish tank, Germaine ordered Constant to return to his former post as her cavalier. Constant and Mrs. Lindsay continued to see each other, even to occasionally make love, as late as 1805. But for the time being Constant remained as enslaved as ever to Germaine. After all, they shared an extremely important bond—their daughter Albertine, whom Constant adored. Moreover, there were moments when Germaine seemed appeased, and an entirely different personality came to the surface to seduce him once again. "How graceful she is!" Benjamin was still writing in 1803. "How affectionate! How devoted! How intelligent!"[170]

Throughout these tortured remnants of her liaison with Constant, Germaine also pursued other romances. There was a handsome young Irish man named O'Brien who never seemed to leave her side throughout the winter months of 1802–1803. In the late spring there appeared a Scotsman, Lord John Campbell, later the seventh Duke of Argyll, who became enamored of her while trying to improve his morale after an unhappy marriage. He was accompanied by a physician, Dr. Robertson, who also fell ardently in love with Germaine, though one cannot be certain he achieved his erotic goals. Throughout June the trio traveled throughout western Switzerland, Germaine acting as guide to the sights and beauties of her native land. Meanwhile another Scottish admirer of Germaine, a Mr. McCulloch, very jealous of Dr. Robertson, had teamed up with one Mr. Christin, a Swiss diplomat in the service of the Tsar, who had long suffered unrequited love for Germaine. McCulloch decided to resolve his rivalry with Dr. Robertson through a duel, and only Germaine's intervention prevented them from possibly murdering each other. By now, Bonaparte's police, ever on the lookout for British and Russian spies, were very alarmed by all these foreigners paying their court to Mme de Staël. Lords Campbell and Robertson left for Germany, where an officer of the French occupation forces came to arrest them. Campbell managed to escape in women's disguise to Vienna, where his doctor followed him. Christin, however, was arrested in Geneva, released upon Germaine's intercession, rearrested upon Bonaparte's special orders, jailed in Paris for over a year, and only freed thanks to the intercession of the Pope. Obliged to flee his native Switzerland in 1805, he spent his remaining thirty-two years in Russia and continued to write Germaine ardent love letters until her death. "I love you more than I ever have loved anyone, more than I have told you, more than I shall ever tell you. . . . During my worst sufferings, your image was always there like a consoling angel."[171] These romantic interludes indicate the degree of passion that, even as she approached the age of forty, the plain, increasingly stout Germaine could still elicit: she retained a genius for sensing what a man wanted to hear, for making a man feel as if she was the only woman who truly understood him.

If she settled quietly ten leagues from Paris, so Germaine was assured in the late summer of 1803, the First Consul would raise no objection. So in mid-September she left Coppet in the company of Mathieu de Montmorency, Auguste, and Albertine—her younger son, Albert, remained in boarding school in Geneva. Her official destination was a small, chilly country house rented from her lawyer, at Maffliers, northeast of Paris. On the day she arrived she wrote a brief note to Bonaparte asking him whether her exile had "lasted long enough" in his eyes, and whether he was "willing to take into consideration certain family reasons which make my return to Paris an absolute necessity."[172] She was pessimistic yet held out enough hope to rent herself a house on the rue de Lille. At that time Bonaparte was again being given highly exaggerated reports from his special spy, Mme de Genlis. That season Germaine's country house, so it was falsely reported to him, had become a particularly busy meeting place for such dissenters as Montmorency and Mme Récamier. In fact, much of Germaine's time, during this particular stay in France, was spent not in socializing, but in untangling the formidable skein of debts her husband had left across Europe. About Paris she could only sigh: "For those who are persecuted," she wrote Joseph Bonaparte, "it is one of the great misfortunes to beg for the air they breathe."[173] The First Consul remained unmoved by her eloquence. He soon informed her that Maffliers was outside the bounds allowed her, and that if she was still there in October his gendarmes would escort her back to Coppet.

Refusing to believe that he would be so brutal, Germaine asked Constant to drop in on Fouché. The threat to Germaine was very real, Fouché warned him. Four gendarmes were indeed about to drop in on her. A few days later Germaine left Maffliers with Albertine to hide, for a few nights, alternately in the houses of two friends, one of whom was Juliette Récamier. Germaine wrote another letter to the First Consul: "Citizen Consul, it is hard to believe that a hero would not be the protection of the weak. . . ." "Let me die in France," she wrote to Joseph Bonaparte, "so long as it's near Paris, and I shall thank him, I shall pray to him as if he were God Himself!"[174] It was too late. On October 13 Bonaparte signed an order commanding Germaine to move to a distance of forty leagues (110 miles) from the capital. Two days later, she was sitting in her drawing room in the company of Mme Junot, wife of the Marshall, and a few other friends, waiting for a messenger from Joseph Bonaparte, who had promised to make one last effort. She had just picked up a bunch of grapes when her guests saw a look of alarm appear on her face. A man on horseback, was ringing the bell of her gate. "They've come to arrest me,"[175] Germaine whispered. She rose to meet her visitor, a lieutenant of the gendarmerie of Versailles who showed her the order signed by the First Consul and treated her with the utmost courtesy. Grapes still in hand, Germaine protested that a woman with two children could not be made to move at twenty-four hours' notice. She needed three days in Paris to put her affairs in order. The lieutenant agreed, as long as he could remain in her company.

At the palace of Saint-Cloud that evening, Marshall Junot appealed again to Bonaparte on Madame de Staël's behalf. "What possible interest can you have in that woman?" Bonaparte cried out, stamping his foot. "An interest that I shall always have in the weak and the suffering, General," Junot replied, "besides, she would worship you if you only let her." "She has only herself to blame," Bonaparte answered. "Let her bear the consequences."[176] Each of Bonaparte's two brothers made one more futile assault, after which they informed Germaine that the First Consul's decision was absolutely irrevocable.

For once Germaine was totally confused about where she should go next: Bordeaux, Lyons, Germany, as she had earlier decided? A note arrived from Joseph to visit him at his home at Marfontaine, and she accepted, finding half of Napoleon's court there, who greeted her with great sympathy. What irony, she thought, to be ostracized by the First Consul, and warmly greeted by his own circle of intimates! Her last possible plea having failed, her passport having arrived, she set out for Metz, on France's eastern frontier, to begin a long journey to Germany. Constant, all his resolutions of independence abandoned in the sight of Minette's distress, had hurried to her side to accompany her. Auguste, Albertine, and two or three servants were also with her. "Farewell!" she wrote her father, having ordered her coach to stop on a hill overlooking Paris, and spent several tearful hours watching the beloved city stretched out before her. "I am about to enter my carriage, three leagues from Paris, seeing it before me, leaving my friends who are there, by force—ah God!" Her letter crossed a note from Necker: "Lift up your head in adversity and never allow anyone, no matter how powerful, to hold you under his boot."[177]

She was beginning her long exile from France, a state of being that for the rest of her life she would compare to the worst of tortures, to a mini-death. Dante, she would remind her readers, "saw exile as a form of hell."[178] She saw exile as a "death in miniature": "One needs less courage to face death than to face exile."[179]

Chapter 12

L'Allemagne

The first time Germaine had been to Germany, in 1796, she did not know a word of German; all she had ever read of German literature was Goethe's *Werther*; and she had only recently become aware of the extraordinary cultural revolution—the Romantic movement—that was transforming Germany in the late eighteenth century. Upon coming home she had been enthused by the writings of a French émigré, Charles de Villers, an eminent Kant scholar who had published a series of essays on the nascence of German Romanticism and later became her friend. She proceeded to take German lessons with her children's tutor and within a year she could read the language fairly well.

Her first stop on this second trip, in December 1803, was Frankfurt. There Albertine came down with a high temperature, which a local doctor misdiagnosed as scarlet fever, informing the family that a girl had died of it a few days earlier in the house next door. Albertine turned out to just have a bad cold, but the misdiagnosis was enough to alarm her mother about Germans' skills. "What a heap of brutality this doctor is!"[180] Germaine wrote her father at Coppet. "I am bored in Germany," eight-year-old Albertine wrote to her grandfather while convalescing, "without Benjamin, who plays with me, neither Mamma or I would know what to do among all these Germans."[181] Within a few days Germaine had acquired a distinct aversion to residents of Frankfurt. Mostly prosaic merchants and bankers, they seemed to lock away their thoughts and feelings, as she put it, "like objects never to be used, even on Sundays," and she equally disliked their "grave and monotonous formality."[182] It led her to make the first of many damning comparisons between French and Germans. "All material objects in Germany are intolerable—beds, food, stoves.... Except for the educated minority, Germans, if judged by French tastes and sensibility, barely belong to the human race."[183] She was so depressed by Frankfurt that she convinced Constant, who had been planning to leave her there, to accompany her to her next destinations, Weimar and Leipzig. During the next few days, traveling through the tiny fairy-tale villages of Thuringia, she found a quite different Germany, which began to move her. She wrote to Villers:

> I had stopped at an inn, in a small town, where I heard the piano being played beautifully in a room which was full of steam from woollen clothes drying on an iron stove: That seems to be true of everything here: there is poetry in their soul but no elegance of form.[184]

Her esteem for Germany grew more when she arrived in Weimar at Christmas time. Three successive German translations of *Delphine* had sold out in the pocket-size duchy, and she was enthusiastically received; Weimarians were anticipating a haughty, high-minded bluestocking, and Duchess Louise, who was not easily charmed, expressed the surprise and enthusiasm of her entire retinue when she characterized Germaine as "unique," forthright and completely unaffected, and "willing to speak with anyone about any subject he is interested in."[185] Rumors that she was a wonderful mother further endeared her to all. Even Germaine's vestments—the colorful turbans, flowing shawls, and daring décolletés ill-suited to her advancing age and much derided by Parisians—were found enchanting. The aging, ardently Francophile dowager duchess, who'd spent her youth adulating Voltaire, particularly delighted in Germaine's company, and when the French visitor recited scenes from Racine's *Andromaque* and *Phèdre* in the duchess's salon her conquest of Weimar high society was complete. Curbing her habitual forthrightness, Germaine had been careful not to express her anti-Bonapartist views—a small court such as Weimar's might have taken umbrage at her opinions. The duke was so impressed with her, in fact, that he summoned the reclusive poets Goethe and Schiller to his court to meet her.

Such eminent intellectuals gave her slightly more cautious reviews. Goethe took a few weeks to warm up to her, at first resenting her very French manner of turning literary discussions into lighthearted bantering: "To philosophize in a social setting means to indulge in lively conversation on insoluble problems, this was her true joy and passion," he commented. "My obstinate contrariness often drove her to despair, but it was then that she was at her most amiable and that she displayed her mental and verbal agility most brilliantly." Schiller found that Germaine represented "French intellectual culture [at its purest]. . . . She wants to explain everything, apprehend everything, measure everything," he commented. "For what Goethe calls poetry she has no sense at all . . . however she never esteems any false values and always recognizes true ones."[186]

These estimations were accurate: Germaine had no ear whatsoever for poetry or music, neither did she have much of an eye for architecture—unfortunate failings for anyone struggling to understand German traditions. But she immediately grasped the richness of Germany's literary culture at that moment of history, and its proliferation of utterly original, revolutionary ideas. Her exchanges with Goethe eventually took on a playful, friendly tone. "Madame de Staël would make a pronouncement on art, and Goethe would be paralyzed with shock," so one observer described a typical meeting. "Then Goethe would make a cutting remark on false sentimentality. . . and Madame de Staël would shake with indignation at such heresy . . . thus the conversational minuet continued."[187] In March 1804, after many weeks of discoursing with Goethe and other Weimar luminaries, Germaine and her entourage left for Leipzig.

Both Germaine and Constant were impressed by the richness of the Romantic sensibility they encountered throughout Germany, but Germaine still missed Paris.

"All this gives me release from pain, but no real pleasure," she wrote her father, "pleasure would be love, or Paris, or power. I need one of these three things in order to exalt my heart, my mind, my activity"[188] "Ah! The gutters of the rue du Bac!"[189] she may have mused as she stood before treasures of German Gothic and baroque architecture, blind to their beauty. (Her retinue passed by the cathedral of Naumburg, which displays some of the greatest treasures of Gothic sculpture—without even entering it.) After three days in Leipzig—nothing much to do there beyond calls to a few booksellers and professors—Constant was scheduled to return to France, and she suddenly felt plagued by her habitual dread of solitude. Constant, too, was filled with affection for his old friend, and she even extracted from him the promise never to marry another woman. "There is no more kind, loving, intelligent, and devoted creature,"[190] he wrote in his diary the day they parted.

Germaine's stay in Berlin was her most triumphant to date. She was invited to the birthday ball of Queen Louise of Prussia, an occasion for which she had a new dress run up in twenty-four hours. "I have admired you for a long time," the queen said to Germaine after the formal presentations, "and have been impatient to make your acquaintance."[191] The Berlin press quoted those very words. Would Bonaparte ever hear them? Germaine wondered. Would he ever be moved by the enthusiastic reception she was getting throughout the German principalities, kingdoms, duchies? She stayed in Berlin for a few weeks and, welcomed as an Ambassadress of the French Spirit, shared every single meal with a prince, a duke, an ambassador, or a distinguished writer. But she so missed Paris that notwithstanding these festivities she felt time was rushing by "joylessly." "Society in the large cities of Germany imitates Paris, and Paris in German loses a great deal in translation,"[192] she wrote to Joseph Bonaparte. Moreover, she disliked Berlin because its intellectuals did not cultivate the art of conversation and kept their thoughts to themselves (a habit she did not exactly practice).

In terms of its permanent impact on her life, the highlight of Germaine's stay in Berlin was her meeting with August Wilhelm Schlegel, a scholar who had been introduced to her by Goethe, and whom she had chosen to be her mentor in her studies of German culture. Schlegel, thirty-six years old, trilingual in French, English, and German, had acquired great literary distinction as a critic and translator and was particularly noted for having been the first to translate Shakespeare's plays—sixteen of them—into German. It is through Schlegel, in fact, that Shakespeare became part of the German literary heritage: his translations would remain unmatched for generations and are still read today. Schlegel's personality, it should be noted, direly lacked the sparkle of his intellect: this "pedant of romanticism," as he has been called, was a small, ugly, vain, quarrelsome man—faults only barely surmounted, in the opinion of some, by his great brilliance. Schlegel had been divorced for some years before he met Germaine, and after a few impressive meetings with him Germaine indulged in one of her odder whims: she brought him back to France to be her children's tutor. It seems curious that someone of Schlegel's intellectual eminence would accept such a position; but he was as poor and as snobbish as he was prominent, and he was drawn by the prospect that Madame de Staël could introduce him to Europe's most distinguished persons. Moreover—couldn't one have guessed it?—he had fallen in love with Germaine.

By this time, Bonaparte had crowned himself Emperor of the French, ruling as Napoleon I. And Germaine's stay in Berlin was made complex by the news of Napoleon's having abducted and murdered Louis XVI's cousin, the Duke d'Enghien, who after the Revolution had sought refuge in Germany. Torn between its awe of the Emperor and its anger at this crime against a person of royal blood, the Prussian court expected Germaine to take a stand on the tragedy. Germaine, who for once was managing to remain diplomatic, was unwilling to publicly attack Napoleon and resolved her dilemma by making plans to leave Berlin. But she would leave it even earlier than she'd thought. On the evening of April 18, Germaine received a message demanding that she instantly return to Coppet: her father was very ill. She immediately packed her bags and placed Schlegel in her carriage; the two seldom parted again.

Necker died the day after he'd fallen ill, and upon this particular crisis Constant showed himself to be a man of duty. He realized that only he could bring Germaine the news of her father's death, that if borne by any other messenger it could have a catastrophic impact on her. As she sped home from Berlin he sped to wait for her at Weimar. He gave her the news, and her reaction was even more violent than he had feared. Schlegel was present at the scene:

"She fell to the ground with a piercing scream, they had to hold her arms tightly to prevent violent movements, she continued screaming as if she had lost her reason. . . . We had arrived [in Weimar] at half past four, and only at nine o'clock did she calm down a little. . . . She never ceased reproaching herself bitterly for her journey and her absence. . . . I kept vigil. She was incapable of closing her eyes for a few seconds without starting up convulsively. Only at dawn did she sleep for a quarter of an hour."[193]

She remained at Weimar for nine days to restore and calm herself. On the journey home, Constant and Schlegel took turns reading aloud to her. The triad resorted easily to quarrels and emotional outbursts. Constant was suddenly jealous of Schlegel, sensing that the latter had fallen in love with his Minette. He relieved his anxiety in Bern by finding a brothel. Schlegel, ultrasensitive about any literary issues, started weeping when speaking of Cervantes. As the coach approached Coppet Germaine became convulsive. A large crowd of villagers had turned out for her arrival. The carriage thundered into the cobblestoned courtyard, and as it came up to the door of the manor, Schlegel writes, she "fell out of the carriage. . . . Never in my life have I heard a more piercing scream than when she was carried by her servants, half unconscious, into her house."[194]

Germaine spent much of the summer of 1804 reading and filing her father's papers. It may have served her as that ritual of mourning we must all undertake to psychically survive our great losses. She collected those writings of Necker's she loved best and had them published in Geneva with her own preface, in which she eulogized her father rather outlandishly (she compared his writings to Voltaire's). "I had lost in that absence my protector, my brother, my friend, the man I would have chosen as my life's unique companion, if destiny had not thrown me into a generation other than his!" she wrote.[195] "Nothing seemed beyond remedy as long as he lived," Germaine also wrote in the last pages of her essay, "Du Caractère de M. Necker, et de sa vie privée." "Only since his death have I known true terror; only since then have I lost the confidence of youth, which always relies on its own strength to attain all desires."[196] It was her way of saying that only with her father's death did she truly enter into adulthood.

Was Necker's death a turning point in Germaine's life? Curiously not. She had long ago developed a sense of duty to society that was far more militant than his. What was unexpected about her behavior, from then on, was the extreme wisdom and prudence with which she managed her inheritance, which she looked on as a "sacred trust,"[197] and which she wished to "piously transmit to my children." "I do not want the fruits of such a man's labors to be destroyed." As a result she left her children more than she had been left by her father. Though her way of life was lavish, her personal needs were fairly frugal—her clothing was haphazard, she had no jewelry worth mentioning, and she kept count of every penny. The only true impact of Necker's death on his daughter is that it intensified her innate characteristics. She became more readily panicked about her love affairs, more distressed than ever about the banishment imposed on her by Napoleon, more anxiously in need of being constantly surrounded by friends.

In 1804 she stayed at Coppet for the entire summer, and as its châtelaine, ushered in what has been called "the great days of Coppet"—the 1804–1810 period of that spirited community. During those years Germaine's family home was Europe's principal center of anti-Bonapartist opposition. It was also a permanent seminar and debating society, with an unusually large cast of personalities inhabiting a splendid domain.

For life at Coppet was in every possible manner maintained on a grand scale. The kitchen personnel alone consisted of at least fifteen servants (one can still visit the spacious, sunny kitchen, barely changed since the early nineteenth century, whose stove is surmounted by an array of twelve gleaming copper pans of different sizes in which Germaine's meals were cooked). In summer, the table was laid for thirty guests at each meal. Breakfast was between 10 and 11 a.m., dinner was served at about 5 p.m., followed by an evening drive or by games or music. At 11 supper was served, but for Germaine and her intimates—many of them were, like her, insomniacs—conversation lasted until the morning hours. The guests' schedule was curiously nomadic. There was no fixed space for any particular time of day, the doors to all the rooms were always open, and according to one frequent visitor, "whenever a conversation developed, one set up camp and stayed for hours . . . talking seemed to be everybody's chief business."[198] Second to conversation, amateur theatricals were the favorite pastime. They were open to the public, and strangers came to Coppet from Geneva, Berne, or Lausanne to see Germaine, Juliette Récamier, Benjamin Constant, and August Wilhelm Schlegel in the cast. There have been mixed reports about Germaine's general gifts as a tragedienne, but she is said to have been marvelous in the great Racinian roles, particularly in the jealousy scene of *Phèdre*.

There were village rituals, too, for Germaine was beloved by the locals. Each time she returned from a journey she was welcomed by a band concert in the park. The sick and underprivileged of the village depended much on her charity. On Sundays she never failed to attend the old Gothic church in the village for Protestant service. Her circle of intimates—Constant, the children, and their tutors, including Schlegel—composed the household's inner core. Shortly after Necker's death, they were joined by Jean Charles de Sismondi, a writer and economist seven years Germaine's junior, yet another member of Germaine's circle who was genuinely smitten with her. The author of a popular and highly respected book on economics, *On Commercial Wealth*, Sismondi would not marry until the age of forty-six, two years after Germaine's death, and wrote upon her passing that "it is all over with this vivifying society, this magic lantern of the world, which . . . has taught me so much. There is no one to whom I owe more than to her."[199] Upon first arriving at Coppet, where he'd looked forward to being alone with Germaine, Sismondi was dismayed to find Constant there running the house—apparently his hostess had not even mentioned him. Any sense of rivalry he might have had toward Constant, however, was allayed by the fact that the two men had a conspiratorial bond created by a mutual pet peeve: they both detested the fussy, hypochondriac, arrogant, humorless Schlegel, who, made all the more argumentative by his insecurity, constantly ran down France and extolled Germany; he was disliked by all of Coppet's inhabitants with the exception of Germaine's children, who had a tolerant, teasing relationship with him. (Reflecting on Sismondi's unfulfilled passion for Germaine, it is interesting to note that with the exception of Constant, Germaine never fell truly in love except with aristocrats. It was not only a matter of elitism: she most loved men who had a certain elegant recklessness, dash, and daring, such as Talleyrand and Narbonne.)

Outside of Germaine's intimate family circle, no visitor to Coppet was more loyal than Juliette Récamier. A note on Juliette—certainly the closest woman friend Germaine ever had—is in order. Jeanne-Françoise-Julie de Récamier, daughter of a Paris lawyer, was married at the age of fifteen, at the height of the Reign of Terror, to a wealthy Parisian banker twenty-seven years her senior. She opened the first salon to be held in Paris after the Revolution and infused those gatherings with her own incomparable grace. A small, delicate woman with a timid, whispering voice, she adopted a manner at once frigidly chaste and playfully coquettish; her appearance was comely rather than beautiful: pert oval face, pearly teeth, incomparably radiant skin. And for forty years her mysterious magnetism bewitched many distinguished men and women, eliciting their slavish devotion. She was the great fashion icon of her time, her neoclassical style of dress having imposed a deliberate austerity upon the tastes of the Directory and of the early imperial years. She only wore severe white Grecian tunics, made famous by David's portrait of her; her hair was gathered upward in the antique style, fastened with a girlish ribbon; one pearl bracelet, or a cameo, was the only ornament she ever wore. Few dictators of style have better exemplified the motto "less is more."

The secret of Juliette's seduction lay in her strategies of refusal and resistance. There is ample proof that her alliance with Récamier was a "white" marriage, never physically consummated because of her dread of sexuality and her husband's decision to "respect her sensibilities." Although Juliette's maidenly grace exerted an irresistible attraction on men, she would remain a virgin until her forties, when she began a liaison with Chateaubriand that lasted until her death. Juliette's numerous suitors discovered that falling in love with this goddess of chaste seduction, who flirted with virtually every man she knew, playing with passion but terrified of surrendering to it, could be an infernal experience. It may well be Germaine's masculinity—the "man/woman" aspect of her personality, as Constant put it—that appealed to Juliette when they first met in 1805. The two started a passionate friendship, marked by a correspondence of great ardor, and conversations in which each woman brought out the best elements of the other's intelligence. "If it is possible to envy one whom I love," Mme de Staël wrote her friend, "I would willingly give all that I am in order to be you. Beauty that is unequaled in Europe, a spotless reputation, a proud and generous nature—Dear Juliette, may our friendship grow closer, may this be no longer just a matter of your kindness, but a sustained relationship, a mutual need to confide our thoughts to one another, a life together.... Adieu, my angel, adieu."[200] The tender friendship between the two women often led mutual acquaintances to refer to them as "The Beauty and the Mind." "Here I am seated between the mind and the beauty," a gauche Parisian gent once exclaimed as he plunked himself down on a sofa between them. "That is the first time I've ever been referred to as a great beauty,"[201] Germaine replied with aplomb.

But it was only in 1807, after the death of her cherished mother, that Juliette was finally able to accept Germaine's numerous offers to spend the summer at Coppet. One can still visit her room at the château, a small, virginal white chamber right next to Germaine's larger, more ornate, predominantly red bedroom. Along with Juliette came her retinue of admirers: Prince August of Prussia, mad with love for the beauty; Mr. Middleton, a wealthy American art student; the German philanthropist Baron von Vogt, equally smitten; two

Russian admirers, Baron Balk and Prince Tuffiakin; and the eminent writer Francois René de Chateaubriand, who would eventually be the great love of Juliette's life. Add to those houseguests, for a typical Coppet mix, Mme Vigée Le Brun, the statesman Francois Guizot, the Duchess of Courland, and the German mystic Mme de Krudener, who made a few recruits at Germaine's court but was never able to convert the hostess. In sum, a good part of Europe's aristocrats and literati passed through Coppet. The intensity of its discourse was well described by Charles-Victor de Bonstetten, a historian and writer who spent whole winters there with Germaine in the company of Mathieu de Montmorency and Constant. "I just returned from Coppet," he wrote, "and I feel completely stupefied . . . and exhausted by the intellectual debauches," he wrote Mme Vigée Le Brun. "More wit is expended at Coppet in a single day than in many a country during a whole year."[202]

Over time, the triumvirate of friends who had been the closest companions of Germaine's youth— Narbonne, Talleyrand, and Mathieu de Montmorency— was reduced to one: the first two had chosen to wield power under the Emperor, and only Montmorency, who made his entire family swear that they would never serve Napoleon, remained a faithful member of her circle. But Montmorency was much occupied by his country estate. So it was Schlegel, *faute de mieux*, who was Germaine's principal traveling companion and accompanied her to Italy in 1805, shortly after he had entered her service. He grew sorrowful when Sismondi joined them midjourney, and upon their return grew even more jealous when he saw that Constant was still at Coppet. Schlegel wrote Germaine a long desolate letter complaining about "the noisy solitude" of Coppet, reminding her that he had left his family and his fatherland for her, and was desolate to find that her passions had long been taken up with other men. Germaine, terrified that he would leave, engaged him in one of her all-night talk-fests, which she must have handled well enough, for the following morning she received the following communication from her new slave: "I declare that you have every right over me and that I have none over you. Dispose of my person and of my life, command, refuse—I will obey you in everything. . . . I am proud of being your property . . . you have a supernatural power over me which I would not struggle against in vain."[203]

Schlegel kept his word until her death. Much as Germaine's captives might rage at her, most of them remained in her thrall, and however they might hate each other there was a weird brotherhood among them. When Germaine went to Geneva for the day, for example, Constant dined with Bonstetten, Sismondi, and Schlegel "like schoolboys when the master of studies is away." "Strange woman!" he wrote in his diary that day. "She exerts over everything around her a kind of inexplicable but very real power. If she could govern herself, she might have governed the world."[204]

Chapter 13

Corinne

The trip Germaine took with Schlegel to Italy in 1805 provided the principal inspiration for her most famous work, the novel *Corinne, ou L'Italie,* which would be published in 1807. During that journey, she was very critical, in her letters, about the lack of social cohesiveness in the Italian peninsula—"Everywhere there is a mixture of wealth and poverty, of love for the fine arts and of bad taste, of education and ignorance, of greatness and pettiness—in a word, this is not a nation, because there is no coherence . . . no vigor in its life."[205] "Ridicule is unknown [here], since there is no society." She traveled through the northern part of Italy visiting its monuments—palaces, churches, museums—and paying little attention to what she saw. What interested her more were the honors she received, such as being lionized by the Roman aristocracy or being made an honorary member of the Academia dell' Arcadia.

But then she got to Rome, and she fell passionately in love with it. "What attracts me in this city is a mystery that does not reveal itself on first acquaintance, a sensation of the South that is completely unknown to those who have not been there, a certain sympathy between nature and man that can not be imagined anywhere else. . . . "[206]

In point of fact, Germaine had also fallen in love with a handsome local resident, Dom Pedro de Souza e Holstein, a melancholy, reserved diplomat of Portuguese origins. Aged twenty-four, he may have thought it a novel experience to be cherished by a woman of genius fifteen years older than he. He let himself be swept along to Naples in the company of Germaine's entire menagerie—Schlegel, Sismondi, Albertine. Germaine found Naples even more overpowering than Rome. ("As you approach Naples, you experience a sensation of absolute well-being."[207]) She explored at length the neighboring ruins of Pompeii and even ascended Vesuvius at night in a carriage as Dom Pedro rode his horse at her side, watching the luminous river of lava flowing "like a tiger, stealthily, with measured steps."[208] Although she enjoyed the city, she deplored the Neapolitans' lack of dignity, finding them to be "in certain respects, not even a civilized race."[209] She much enjoyed the royal court, however, where Queen Marie-Caroline, Marie-Antoinette's sister, welcomed her warmly and spent several hours alone with her. Germaine boasted much about this visit in a letter to Hochet, seemingly unconcerned that it might be reported to the Emperor of France, who looked on Marie-Caroline as one of his worst enemies and whom he was about to depose from her throne.

As for Dom Pedro, Germaine was realistic about the potentially short duration of their liaison. There were aspects of his character—a passive reserve, among other traits—she came to resent. "Everything I feel, I say; your feelings are hidden by a veil,"[210] she lashed out in one of her letters. Yet notwithstanding his inertness Dom Pedro served an extremely important purpose: She found in him some crucial character traits she needed to fill out the portrait of Oswald, the protagonist of her novel *Corinne*, which would make her Europe's most famous writer.

Staël's heroine Corinne (into whom the author once more pours many of her own characteristics) is an Anglo-Italian poetess with mysterious origins, famous for her talent as an improviser, and gifted in all the arts. A Scottish peer currently visiting Italy, the melancholy, repressed Oswald, Lord Nelvil, is struck with admiration when he meets her at Rome's Capitol, where she has just given a triumphal performance. To allay Oswald's despondency and his distrust of the sensuality and exuberance of Italy, Corinne guides him through Rome and the surrounding countryside, teaches him about the art and the history of the peninsula, and tries to instill in him her own love for the country.

But each of the lovers is hiding a secret from the other. As they visit Vesuvius and stare at its rivers of glowing lava, Oswald tells Corinne of his recent unhappy love for a perfidious French woman: she retained him in France against the wishes of his father, Lord Nelvil, who died without seeing his son again. Oswald is filled with guilt because he had not obeyed his father's dying wish—for him to eventually marry one Lucile Edgermond, who turned out (unbeknownst to him at the time of his father's death) to be Corinne's half-sister. Corinne then tells Oswald her side of the story: her Italian mother died when she was an infant. Her British father, Lord Edgermond, had remarried a woman who proved to be a mean, glacial stepmother; he had wanted Corinne to marry the son of his best friend. But the friend had found the bold, extravagantly gifted Corinne to be so different from the demure, reserved wife he wished for his son that he changed his mind. Corinne remained single, supporting herself by her great talents.

Very moved by Corinne's tale, Oswald swears he will be faithful to her. But soon afterward he begins to waver, for his father's family and other members of his social milieu have been spreading rumors about Corinne's dubious morality. Disillusioned and doubting Corinne's capacity for fidelity, Oswald goes back to England, falls in love with Lucile Edgermond, Corinne's half-sister, and in accordance to his father's earlier wishes, marries her.

Corinne, aware of Oswald's innocent treachery and moved by Lucile's pure and selfless love for him, decides to sacrifice herself to the couple's happiness. She returns to Rome, finds that her former talents have vanished and declines into despair.

After a few years of a very dull, unhappy marriage, Oswald and Lucile visit Italy in the company of their daughter and find Corinne close to death. She forgives them both on her deathbed and tries to reunite them. Like *Delphine,* but to a far greater degree, *Corinne* explores the issue of superior women confronted and ultimately destroyed by a prejudiced society—a society exemplified, in both novels, by an intelligent, generous, but overly conventional man.

There are grandiose themes in this book that reach far beyond its plot. The contrast between the Nordic, reserved Oswald and the expansive, meridional Corinne allows Germaine to expound at length on the differences between the Northern and Southern psyches and between Classicism and Romanticism (Germaine is credited by many critics for having coined that latter term). The novel's impact was manifold. It gave its French readers vast amounts of information about the history and landscape of Italy, which were as unknown to the French as the basic facts of German culture had been; it initiated an ardent cult of Italy among France's budding Romantic writers and its public at large—the Marquis de Sade was as great a fan as Germaine had. And it had considerable impact on women readers outside of France, offering a utopia of female independence that they dearly wished to emulate: Corinne lives alone on her own money, never deferring to her family. She goes into society without a protector or an escort; her friends and lovers are of her own choosing; she publishes, exhibits, performs, and is famous in her own right—she guides her own life in every possible sense. Among her fans outside of France were Mary Godwin, author of *Frankenstein,* who read *Corinne* while nursing the baby she had with Shelley; George Eliot's Maggie Tulliver, heroine of *The Mill on the Floss,* reads and discusses *Corinne* at some length; even Harriet Beecher Stowe felt "intense sympathy" for Corinne.

Once again, Germaine was naive enough to hope that her book's vast success would impress the Emperor and lead him to be more tolerant of her. How wrong she was. Germaine's critical attitude toward the French, and her love for England, were clearly revealed in the way *Corinne* contrasts the generosity of the warmhearted British Oswald with the frivolity of Corinne's other suitor,

a vapid Frenchman named Comte d'Erfeuil. Napoleon
was particularly irritated by the book. He sent orders to
wake up Talleyrand in the middle of the night and asked
him to read him some pages of *Corinne* aloud. After a
half hour he cut him off, saying "this is no sentiment, it's
a hash of phrases! Go to bed, we're wasting our time."[211]
And he again ordered Germaine's book to be denounced
as "anti-French" throughout the government-run press.
Napoleon was also boorish enough to suggest, through
the mediation of Police Minister Fouché, that if Mme de
Staël was willing to insert into the next edition of *Corinne*
a few laudatory remarks on the Emperor, he would
return the two million her father had loaned to France
on the eve of the Revolution.[212] Germaine, appalled,
said that she was willing to remove any material from
the book the government found offensive but refused
to insert a word of flattery. Shortly afterward, hearing
that Germaine, unaware that her every step was watched,
had ventured into Paris after dark, Napoleon, now holed
up in his tent in the battlefields of East Prussia, dashed
off the following words of reprimand to Fouché: "It is
my intention that she never leave Geneva. . . . It truly
is difficult to restrain one's indignation at the spectacle
of all the political metamorphoses this whore, and an
ugly one at that, is causing."[213] The Emperor's rage at
Corinne helped the book sell all the more spectacularly
throughout Europe.

While Germaine had been writing *Corinne*, she had
found yet another whiff of inspiration for the creation
of her fictional character Oswald in the person of one

Prosper de Barante, of whom she became very enamored. An official of the Ministry of the Interior ten years her junior, he was distinguished by his elegance, intelligence, and delicate health. After two months of his first stay at Coppet he had become intimate enough with Germaine to address her the following note: "Adieu. I embrace you and I love you. . . . Sometimes when I hold you in my arms, I regret that I am not able to be yours completely. But . . . I tell myself that . . . I need nothing more to declare myself yours forever."[214]

The phrase "not being able to be yours completely" probably refers to Barante's offer of marriage—it is evident from other letters that he had proposed to her, and that she had refused him. Yet Barante clung on at Coppet throughout the winter, notwithstanding its sizable company of swains: in the first months of 1806 he found himself in the company of Constant; Schlegel (who looked at him, he complained, with "ridiculous hatred"[215]); that other infatuated scholar, Sismondi; and Dom Pedro. Barante left Coppet to assume his government duties the following April. At the end of that month Germaine, in hot pursuit of him, arrived at Auxerre, some 100 kilometers from Paris, where she had rented a house for the summer, and immediately summoned all her close friends to join her. Juliette Récamier, Mathieu de Montmorency, and a few others readily arrived, but the most urgent demand was sent to Barante, who was more reluctant. Like her other lovers, he had begun to realize that her demand for love exceeded his capacity.

To make life even more complicated, by the end of the summer Prosper de Barante, weary of Germaine's exuberant possessiveness, had begun to long for the quiet, retiring Juliette Récamier. Germaine's relationship with Barante would reach its nadir in the summer of 1807, upon the publication of *Corinne*. She sent him the three-volume work, and he reacted with indignation. "I want no part of Oswald, I think he is cold-hearted and unimaginative," he wrote, "... you have imprisoned me in that Oswald, in whom I am powerless to defend myself.... I told you some time ago how upset my life was as a result of having known you.... Ah, do not speak to me of applause and success, you who have lived it, who have sought it in every way, who are not afraid of making books out of the most intimate experiences of the heart, of things that are so personal that a modicum of modesty should forbid their use as an instrument of obtaining success."[216]

Another of Germaine's romantic crises in those years had to do with Constant's infatuation with one Charlotte Von Hardenberg, with whom he'd had a brief flirtation a decade earlier, and who had divorced her husband out of love for the writer. They resumed their romance shortly before Constant's fortieth birthday, and she allowed him to possess her. A few weeks later, when Germaine was in a particularly desperate mood because Barante had been posted to a government job in Spain, she walked into Constant's room and read a passionate love letter he had just written to Charlotte. Constant related in his journal that Germaine's resulting tantrum lasted "without interruption throughout the entire day and the entire night."[217] In the following months Constant continued to live at Coppet, furtively meeting with Charlotte on rare occasions. After Charlotte sought his pity by faking a grave illness, the tortured pair was married. It would have been impossible to hide this fact from Germaine, and the couple wrote her a long letter. Germaine then summoned Charlotte to come alone to Coppet by herself and held her captive for one of her 10 p.m. to 4 a.m. discussions, during which she remained, according to Charlotte, surprisingly and consistently "gentle."

Germaine focused her rage, instead, on Constant. After calming her wrath about his marriage and promising that he would not make it public for some months, Constant resumed his habitual life at Coppet, keeping his wife at a safe distance. One morning, Charlotte, understandably irked by her husband's long absences, swallowed a large dose of laudanum and urgently summoned him to her side—"Hurry, hurry, I wish to see you one more time!" Constant arrived in time to rescue her, and a few days later, after she'd been restored to health, he returned to Coppet to resume his usual routine there. From then on, Charlotte became resigned to Constant's indissoluble bond with Germaine and ceased most histrionics.

In the fall of 1806, as Germaine was putting the finishing touches on *Corinne* in the house she had rented at Rouen, Constant was working in a white heat on his novel *Adolphe*. One of the gems of French nineteenth-century literature, its heroine, Ellénore, was a blend of Charlotte, his former lover Anna Lindsay, and Germaine. The themes of *Corinne* and *Adolphe* are similar: Both heroines are victimized by the hero's pathetic inability to ever make a forthright, valiant decision. Constant finished *Adolphe* in a few weeks but did not publish it for another ten years. He had the temerity, however, to read it aloud to Germaine one night, and he suffered the consequences. Germaine could not tolerate the thought that he had merged her—her, *the* unique Germaine de Staël—with such vapid commonplace females as Charlotte and Anna Lindsay. "Unexpected scene because of the novel," he wrote the following day. "These scenes now cause me physical pain, I coughed blood."[218] According to Constant, Germaine's tantrums concerning *Adolphe* were repeated for four consecutive nights, until the opening of a new year, January 1807.

The enthusiasm with which *Corinne* was received throughout Europe somewhat cheered Germaine during her return to Coppet that spring ("*Corinne* is an immortal book," Elizabeth Barrett Browning wrote, "and deserves to be read three score and ten times—that is once every year in the age of man."[219]). Coppet was fuller than it ever had been before: the guests' time was spent in various cheerful activities, such as boat outings on the lake, musical evenings, festive dinners, theatrical rehearsals and performances, and varied excursions, the most arduous of which was Germaine's and Juliette's failed attempt to climb the Mont Blanc together. (Their décolletés were burned to a crisp before they even reached the bottom of the glacier.) But the Coppet community had its serious side. A gathering place for the crème de la crème of the European intelligentsia, similar to what Ferney had been in Voltaire's time, it was the

Continent's most cosmopolitan and influential salon, a literary coterie in which novel ideas sprang up that would influence the rest of the century. It was one of the few places where the Emperor was looked on as a criminal rather than a mere tyrant. And this consensus on the part of eminent writers and intellectuals had a powerful influence on public opinion throughout Europe.

Constant had remained in Paris for two months after Germaine left for Coppet, whence threatening letters arrived daily (Germaine was dying, she would kill herself through an overdose of opium and let it publicly be known that Constant had slain her). He wavered, as tortured and indecisive as ever, and to bide time went to stay with his father at Dôle. Shortly after he'd sought refuge there, Schlegel arrived, letting Benjamin know that if he did not immediately return to Coppet Mme de Staël would come to Constant, swallow poison, and die at his feet. After a violent argument with Schlegel, Constant finally promised to return to Coppet with him. Germaine was waiting for them in the courtyard as they arrived after a twenty-four hour trip; and as Constant stepped out of the carriage she dragged him a few hundred meters away and shouted out every insulting thought that had come to her mind during his absence. Constant wisely kept absolute silence. ("Lamentations, resigned answers on my part, her fury at my resignation, and then the constant menace 'I shall kill myself.'" he wrote in his journal.)[220] In the next few days Germaine, though calmed by her tantrum, daily continued to broadcast her threat to end her life.

In August, Benjamin, more desperately confused than ever about what direction his life should take, wrote Germaine a letter telling her that he was leaving for good and would never see her again. Then he tore up the letter, went to her room, and ordered her to marry him right then and there. (It is useless to ever attempt making sense of Constant's states of mind.) "Her fury," he wrote later, "was as great as her surprise." She called her children in. "Behold the man who wants to ruin your mother and compromise your future by forcing her to marry him!"[221] she said. As the puzzled youngsters, who adored Constant, looked on, Germaine threw herself on the floor and tried to strangle herself with her scarf. After he'd calmed her with soothing words Constant retired to his room to write her yet another letter—which this time he did not tear up—to say that he was leaving and would never return. At dawn of the following morning he put the letter on her desk and crept out of Coppet. He sought refuge in Lausanne with a relative and sat up in a state of terror, waiting for the inevitable: a few hours later there was Germaine, invading the house, throwing herself at Constant's feet and shouting invectives at his relatives, whom she accused of hiding him from her. He ultimately acceded to her demands that he grant her two more months, and that same evening he was back at Coppet.

On November 1, 1807 Constant's promised stay was up. But he was so absorbed by the writing of a play—*Walsein,* an adaptation of Schiller's tragedy *Wallenstein*—that he had no desire to leave Coppet before it was finished; Germaine, as usual, was giving him invaluable advice. Indifferent to the tearful letters he received from Charlotte, who for a month had been waiting for him at an inn in Besançon, Constant doggedly continued his work until Germaine left for Vienna in the company of her usual retinue: Schlegel, Albert, Albertine, and her factotum, Uginet. Constant accompanied her until Lausanne. As he sat in his carriage on his return trip through the Jura mountains, he penned the following thought in his diary about his many abortive attempts to escape Germaine: She had been "the tyrant, but also the goal of my life." By leaving her, he added, he would "cast out all the good I might have done during more than one-third of my existence."[222] As his carriage approached Besançon, there followed a typical Constant scene: Charlotte and her maid waited for him a mile from town, standing by the road. By way of greeting, Benjamin raged at his wife, saying she should have at least come to wait for him in a carriage. Charlotte meekly told him to continue in his own carriage, while she trudged back to the inn on foot. Benjamin reached his destination an hour ahead of his wife, and according to his diary, during that interval of time he wrote Germaine "the most passionate love letter . . . [she] ever received from me."[223]

As his mother was reaching Vienna in the company of his siblings and Schlegel, Auguste de Staël, now seventeen, went to Chambéry, where Napoleon was currently staying, to fulfill a mission assigned him by his mother. Germaine was hoping that Napoleon would finally grant her a residence permit in Paris, as well as the return of two million francs owed her for some twenty years by the French government; and she gambled on the possibility that Auguste's youth and charm might sway the Emperor. But before Auguste had even had a chance to present his requests, Napoleon, just finishing lunch, launched into a tirade against Auguste's grandfather, Jacques Necker, whom he referred to as "an ideologue, a madman, an old maniac." "It was he who led the king to the scaffold. . . . He was responsible for the Revolution. . . . Yes, I tell you that even Robespierre, Marat, Danton have done less harm to France than M. Necker."[224] Although terrified, Auguste then jumped in and pleaded with the Emperor to end his mother's exile. Napoleon stepped up to the young man and tweaked his ear—a sign of favor he gave his favorite soldiers. "Far from offending me, your frankness pleases me," he said. "I like a son who pleads his mother's cause."[225] The Emperor went on to explain all the reasons why Mme de Staël would never be allowed to live in Paris. "Paris is . . . where I live. I don't want anyone there who doesn't like me." But his mother's central interest was literature, Auguste pleaded. "Women should stick to knitting,"[226] the Emperor lashed out after saying that literature and politics were closely allied. And he ended the interview, leaving the room with a brief salute.

Later that year Napoleon's hatred for Germaine found a new outlet: the harassment of her sons. The Ecole Polytéchnique had just been founded by the Emperor (it remains, to this day, one of the three most prestigious graduate schools in France—a blend of Harvard and MIT). And Auguste de Staël passed the entrance exams with flying colors. But although Auguste and his brother were born in France, Bonaparte blocked his access to the school, as he would his brother's, on the grounds that they were foreigners.

Shortly after Auguste's interview with the Emperor, Germaine arrived in Vienna, where she was disliked by most members of that city's ultraconformist and militantly pro-Bonapartist society. They could not forget that she had backed a Revolution that had led their Emperor's aunt to the guillotine. Moreover, they could not forgive her admittedly outlandish attire. "Her clothes were ridiculous to the highest degree," a local citizen wrote, "and rendered her natural ugliness even more hideous."[227] With age Germaine had indeed grown stouter, her features coarser. Her chin had receded, giving more prominence to her large, widely spaced teeth. Her skin color had turned sallow, and the abundant rouge she used to hide the discoloration did not help. Moreover, as if denying that she was well into her forties, she continued to bare her increasingly thick arms and ruddy chest under the low-plunging décolletés of shrill-hued dresses, and to adorn her head with the outlandish paraphernalia of her youth—turbans surmounted by flamboyant bird-of-paradise feathers. Her showy attire, her ceaseless fidgeting with bits of paper or twigs, her stentorian voice: during the months Germaine remained in Vienna, those features made her an object of cruel fun in the city's priggishly elitist social circles.

Vienna's literati received "the whirlwind in petticoats," as one Viennese called her, a tad more kindly. "She is a phenomenon of vitality, egotism, and intellectual activity," wrote Caroline Schelling, Schlegel's former wife. "Her appearance is transfigured by her soul, as indeed it needs to be."[228] Yet however much the Viennese ridiculed Germaine, her fame, and their own snobbism, incited them to invite her to all the great houses—the Liechtensteins, the Furstenbergs, the Esterhazys, the Palffys. Moreover, Germaine's utter lack of self-consciousness—which might indeed have been one of her great sources of strength—made her impervious to any hostility shown her. Or could her indifference to that hostility be traced to the fact that she had once more fallen in love?

The young man's name was Graf Moritz O'Donnell von Tyrconnel, commonly referred to as Maurice O'Donnell. His family, of Irish origins, had settled in Vienna after the fall of the Stuarts. Maurice, who was, typically, eighteen years younger than Germaine, had served as captain in the Corps of Engineers but had resigned in his twenties to lead a life of leisure. From the start, the couple's romance was frequently stalled because Maurice was a bit of a hypochondriac; because Germaine tried to educate the indolent youth, teaching him English and chemistry, to give an aim to his sterile existence; and also because he feared that being seen with a woman old enough to be his mother would make him seem ridiculous. So after a few weeks he found all manner of medical excuses for avoiding Germaine's advances. The impassioned rhetoric that Germaine lavished on all her earlier searches for true love—alternations of imperious demands and tearful lamentations—began all over again. "I beg you on my knees for a hearing . . . it seems to me that every day we draw further apart."[229]

Might it be that Germaine was chronically in love with love, addicted to the vocabulary of infatuation? Might it be that this addiction was linked to her bipolar personality, her inclination to alternate states of exalted joy with crises of despair and disillusionment? In the same weeks that she was mooning over O'Donnell she was writing Constant: "My heart, my life, everything I have is yours if you wish and as you wish. Think about this . . . love me one hundredth as much as I love you."[230]

After two months in Vienna, whatever romantic anguish Germaine was experiencing over O'Donnell was somewhat allayed by the arrival of the faithful Schlegel, who had just written a learned paper comparing Racine's *Phèdre* with Euripides' *Phaedra*. This essay, which Germaine much admired, enabled her to obtain for Schlegel a lecture series concerning dramatic literature, and the addresses had a considerable success (for years to come Schlegel would boast about the fact that it was attended by eighteen princesses).

Germaine left Vienna in May, terrified of losing her O'Donnell, but incited to move by her well-reciprocated distaste for the Viennese. She went on to Dresden, Weimar, Gotha, Frankfurt, and Basel, triumphantly received everywhere, writing O'Donnell from every one of her stops and expecting answers from him as she arrived in each city. None ever came. Her suffering reached its peak when she returned to Coppet and found there a brutal missive from O'Donnell. Its extreme harshness can be traced to the pettiness of Viennese society, which had spread a rumor to the effect that Germaine had refused O'Donnell's offer of marriage. O'Donnell had already been exasperated by her invasive attention to him, and the Viennese fables humiliated him deeply. His letter made it clear that he was breaking off all relations with her and never wished to see her again. Thus ended the last (might some readers join the author in a sigh of relief?) of Germaine's many infatuations. In future years she behaved to O'Donnell, who would rise to the rank of lieutenant general, with great civility: in 1811, when he married Christine de Ligne, she sent him warm congratulations.

During the summer of 1808 Coppet was graced with its habitual crowd of intimates—among them Constant; Sismondi; Baron Voght; Count Kochubey, who had been foreign minister under Tsar Paul I; and the sculptor Friedrich Tieck, who had designed the bas-relief on the Necker family's mausoleum. There was also an esteemed new guest, Zacharias Werner, a German poet and mystic with aspirations of becoming his country's next Schiller. The dinner conversations were more literary than ever—Werner read from his poems; Schlegel from his translations of Shakespeare's *Richard III,* another writer, the playwright Adam Oehlenschläger, from the tragedy he was currently writing. Werner, who was infatuated enough with Germaine to almost come to blows over her with the equally stricken Oehlenschläger, wrote the following description of his hostess:

"She is of middle height, her body, while not slim as a nymph's, is voluptuously beautiful, especially her breast and neck. She is decidedly brunette, and her face is not precisely beautiful, but all criticism is forgotten at the sight of her magnificent eyes through which there shines—nay, flashes with fiery flame—a great, divine soul."[231]

The following winter—that of 1808–1809—may have been the most romantically complex of all Coppet seasons. As Germaine continued to cling to Constant, who was secretly married to Charlotte and thus behaving with unusual meekness, she was still in despair over O'Donnell's treachery and trying to regain the affection of Prosper de Barante, who, in turn, was still infatuated with Juliette Récamier. Juliette, who was also being courted by Prince August of Prussia but was no longer interested in him, was responding with her usual convent-girl coquettishness to Barante's advances. Alarmed, Germaine went so far as to warn Juliette to keep her hands off him: "Don't do it, Juliette. . . . Confiding in you as I do and so prodigiously inferior to your attractions, generosity forbids that you allow yourself the least coquettishness with him."[232] The result of these imbroglios is that Germaine, feeling betrayed by both Barante and Juliette, ceased to correspond with Juliette for over a year. The reconciliation occurred when Juliette, with admirable forthrightness, offered to show Germaine Barante's letters as proof of their chasteness. "Your letter, my dear Juliette, makes me want to throw myself at your feet," Germaine replied. "I do not want to see Prosper's letters—all I want is to be loved by you again."[233] Thus reunited with her dearest friend, Juliette arrived at Coppet in the summer of 1809 and was given her old room, right next to Germaine's. Constant was there as usual, not talking to anyone about his secret marriage, and yet once more preparing to leave Coppet for good. He spent a few weeks mailing small parcels of books and manuscripts he had hoarded at Coppet for the past decade and a half, and then, at dawn one October day, he rode away again.

Constant's return to Coppet, a few months later, shows how truly base his behavior could occasionally be. He had suddenly grown fearful that Germaine might ask him to return the 80,000 francs she had loaned him several years earlier. And in preparation for this particular confrontation, he had engaged in the shoddiest kind of blackmail—spreading detrimental rumors about Germaine in case she might create difficulties over his debt. Germaine, while not pressed for the money, rightly wished Benjamin to pay it back, if only to see him act responsibly, and after some contentious discussions the two reached an agreement: Benjamin signed a paper promising to leave the sum to Germaine in his will, and to include a clause that would bequeath the sum to her children if she did not survive him.

In the winter of 1809 Germaine announced to all her friends that she was leaving for the United States the following summer. Such thoughts of sailing for the New World recurred often in her last decade, whenever she felt most bitter about the geographical taboos imposed upon her by Napoleon and most confused about where to live next. As coolheaded and wise in her dealings with money as she was foolish in her romantic life, she had wisely placed a great deal of her fortune in American investments. And it seemed like a fitting time for her to discover a brand-new country: She was completing the last of the three volumes of her book *De l'Allemagne,* and her publisher, Nicolle, was already producing the first of these volumes at his printing plant in Tours. But she changed her mind, and instead of sailing to America she rented a lovely Renaissance castle a few miles from Tours, Chaumont, to better supervise the printing process. Assembled at Chaumont in addition to her usual court (Schlegel, Mathieu de Montmorency, Juliette, and several of her admirers, etc.) were a musician called Pertosa and a Miss Fanny Randall, a tall, stout, highly educated British spinster with an unhappy past who for the rest of Germaine's life would serve her with fanatic loyalty. Another new addition was one Adelbert von Chamisso, an expatriate French botanist and poet who fell much in love with Germaine, finding that she combined "German seriousness, meridional fire, and French manners."[234] Germaine had to move her "whole caboodle," as she put it, to another castle near Blois, a few miles away, when Chaumont's owner unexpectedly returned from a long trip. At the new residence, Pertosa strummed his guitar and Albertine her harp as they accompanied Juliette's singing of old French songs. The bucolic peace of the household was much shaken, however, by the news that Germaine's old friend, minister of police Fouché, had been dismissed, and replaced by General Savary, a hard-line Bonapartist whose appointment boded ill for the entire company.

As she corrected the last proofs of *De l'Allemagne* in September 1809, Germaine savored her habitual delusions:

the book would so impress the Emperor that her exile might be lifted. Her pride in the book was well grounded. Of Germaine's numerous writings, it is one of four works that can still be read with the greatest pleasure and intellectual benefit, and in this reader's opinion it is the most important of them. (The other three are *On Literature, Considerations on the French Revolution,* and *Ten Years of Exile*). As Germaine's earlier biographer, J. Christopher Herold, has pointed out, *De l'Allemagne* stands midway between Voltaire's *Letters Concerning the English Nation,* published eighty-one years earlier, and Toqueville's *On Democracy in America,* published twenty-two years later. Germaine proceeds by abundantly describing the texture of German society and of its intellectual life, giving vivid accounts of its poets, such as Goethe and Schiller; of its historians and scientists; and of the crowning philosophical achievements of Immanuel Kant. But the book also voices innumerable protests against the stifling of intellectual liberty in contemporary France and frequently condemns a smug, self-satisfied nation that, unlike Germany and England, is absurdly closed to exterior influences and to progressive ideas. ("Have three-quarters of the passages in which she exalts England suppressed,"[235] Napoleon instructed his chief censor after a brief perusal of the book.) Under Napoleon's despotic reign, Germaine intimates without ever once stating the ruler's name, a "silent France" was breeding a new generation of ambitious manipulators and submissive bureaucrats, and the nation's intellectual integrity was being perilously undermined. So the subtext of *De l'Allemagne* was a plea for a revitalization of the French heritage, which could only survive by engaging in a constant process of cross-fertilization with other cultures.

The last and finest chapter, "On the Influence of Enthusiasm," is the key to Germaine's entire philosophy. By enthusiasm, which the Germans possessed to a unique degree, and which the French had lost, she meant the revitalizing energy of deeply felt emotions. A good recording of the "Ode to Joy" of Beethoven's Ninth Symphony and a skilled translation of Schiller's text (as good an example as there is of Germaine's notion of "enthusiasm") might help contemporary readers to deepen their understanding of Germaine's notion of enthusiasm. "Joy, daughter of Elysium,/ Thy magic reunites those/ Whom stern custom has parted./ All men will become brothers/ Under thy gentle wing."

There have been many critical disparagements of *De l'Allemagne* beyond Napoleon's complaint that it was, once again, "anti-French." One might well accuse Germaine of her overly censorious attitude toward the Emperor, who, however despotically he ruled France, introduced a measure of liberalism and equality to several backward countries east of the Rhine and south of the Alps and the Pyrenees. Another accusation—most often made by German critics—is that Germaine's treatment of German literature and philosophy is superficial. That charge is easier to dismiss: Germaine's intention was to present the French reading public, in readily understandable terms, a huge amount of new information about a culture totally foreign to them. Another indictment—the most serious and valid—is that she created an idealized image of

Germany to better condemn Napoleon's suppression of freedom in France. Despite these caveats, *De l'Allemagne,* though occasionally tedious and transparently polemical, is a work in which the contemporary reader can still find a wealth of fascinating observations on nineenth century Europe, on German culture, and, like all worthy books, on the nature of the human condition.

Chapter 14

The Emperor of Matter And the Mistress of Mind

In the early months of 1810, Napoleon instituted a censorship office for all books published in France and placed it under the charge of a friend of Germaine's, Joseph Portalis. This particular censorship policy had many unattractive features, but it did allow most authors to revise their texts before they went to press and make any changes demanded by the censor, thus preventing their works from being seized after publication. By August 1810 Germaine's publisher, M. de Nicolle, had sent the first two volumes of *De l'Allemagne* to the censor, who approved it after subjecting the first volume to minor deletions, which Germaine amiably executed. Unfortunately, M. de Nicolle was a talkative and ambitious man and made the rounds of Paris boasting of a bold and extraordinary book of Mme de Staël's that he was about to publish. Alarmed that rumors about the book would come to the Emperor's attention, Germaine entrusted Juliette Récamier with an important mission: to bring the Emperor a complete set of proofs of all three volumes, along with a personal note. Juliette also carried the proofs of Volume III to one of the censors, the influential poet and academician J. A. Esmenard, who was infatuated, like numerous Parisian men, with Juliette.

But while Juliette was on her way to Paris, Germaine, who was spending some weeks in a village of the Loire region, learned that General Savary, Fouché's successor as head of the French police, had signed a decree ordering Germaine to surrender all proofs and manuscripts of *De l'Allemagne;* Savary's decree also specified that she must leave within forty-eight hours for one of France's Atlantic ports, from which she was to await passage to the United States.

Upon hearing of the Emperor's new offensive—the government destroyed all five thousand copies of the book, along with the typesetters' lead fonts—Germaine acted with unexpected calm. She briefly, quietly wept, and then, while awaiting the official orders, began to round up as many influential friends as possible to help her struggle against the repression of her book. The orders arrived, carried to her by the prefect of the Blois region, a M. Corbigny, who asked her for the manuscript and all the proofs. Gemaine, lying with perfect dignity, gave him an incomplete set of proofs that Corbigny had the gallantry not to examine carefully As for her departure for the United States, she asked for, and received, permission for a week's delay (she ultimately managed to postpone it indefinitely).

In the following days she wrote the Emperor two notes, pointing out that she had proved her loyalty to his regime by trying to have *De l'Allemagne* printed in France, rather than in Germany or Great Britain. She entreated the Emperor to read the manuscript to ascertain for himself whether it contained anything offensive and repeated her plea for an audience with him. She had made all the changes the Chief Censor, M. Portalis, had asked for in the first two volumes and was working on editing the third. What else could she do to conform with his Majesty's decree? But meanwhile, the Emperor had been badgered by innumerable friends of Germaine's, and their persistence, as usual, had taxed his patience. After listening to the plea of Queen Hortense of Holland—Joséphine de Beauharnais' daughter, thus his former stepdaughter—he asked to see the book again. He skimmed it once more for a brief while, became increasingly irritated by what he read and according to one witness, threw it into the fireplace. Shortly thereafter he heard that several copies of the book were still at large in France and fired Prefect Corbigny for incompetence (the official died shortly later, his demise caused, according to his acquaintances, by humiliation and a broken heart).

The triumph of the situation, for Germaine, was that there had always been a well-hidden manuscript of *De l'Allemagne* at Coppet. The faithful Schlegel had spirited it away to Bern, where he kept it in great secrecy. *De l'Allemagne* would be published a year and a half later in Great Britain, to resounding success.

Unaware that she still had some aces up her sleeves, Germaine's friends were astonished by how swiftly her cheer returned after the debacle over her book. She paid back her advance to her publisher, Nicolle, and returned to Coppet, where she resumed the sprightly social schedule she had always enjoyed with her intimates at her family domain. "She is as lively and brilliant as ever," said her childhood friend Catherine Rillet.[236] But her true state of mind, far more complex and melancholy than she would let anyone know, was well expressed in the following words: "Returning to Coppet, like a pigeon with clipped wings. . . . I was resigned to live in my home without ever publishing anything on any subject again. . . . I had to at least find happiness in human affection, and that is the way I arranged my life after I had been stripped of my vocation as a writer."[237]

Censorship policies were not the only ones that had hardened in 1810, when Napoleon's principles of governing grew in every way more repressive. By that time war had been waged throughout Europe for some twelve years. The Emperor had been slow to understand the defiant nationalism affecting the nations he had conquered but had finally grown aware of its potentially explosive force. He responded by instituting far harsher measures on the domestic front. Inmates were held in state prisons without trial; education had to conform to government decrees; the principal purpose of all the arts was to glorify the imperial regime. Fouché's dismissal had been another step in the Emperor's tough new course. The man who replaced him as chief of police, René Savary, Duc de Rovigo, was as brutal and loyal as his predecessor had been subtle and treacherous. "If I ordered Savary to do away with his wife and children," Napoleon once boasted, "I'm sure he would not hesitate."[238] When, in 1810, the Emperor notified Savary that he did not want to hear any more about "that miserable woman" or her book the new police chief took the injunction literally.

He began taking every possible measure to systematically isolate the author of *De l'Allemagne,* and to prevent the book from being published outside France.

Soon after Germaine reached Coppet she was visited by Barante père, Prosper's father, the new prefect of Geneva, and ordered to immediately hand over any proofs of the book that had not yet been given the government. Germaine told Barante that she was not able to return them because they were no longer in Switzerland, and she promised not to have a new edition published on the Continent. Having been presented with this new report, an irate Napoleon also fired Barante from his post and ordered him to withdraw to his estate in the Auvergne. The dismissal of two admired prefects let France's elite know that the battle lines were drawn—its members had either to side with the Emperor, or with Mme de Staël. Much of society still sided with the Emperor, as it had in the earlier incident concerning Constant's rebellious speech at the Tribunate.

Napoleon proceeded on yet another tack: he asked the new prefect of Geneva, Baron Capelle, who had recently been dismissed as prefect of Livorno for having had a romance with Napoleon's sister Elisa, the Grand Duchess of Tuscany, to handle the Staël case. Capelle was led to believe that he might be restored to the Emperor's good graces if he displayed sufficient vigor in his new post. Empress Marie-Louise had just given birth to Napoleon's first heir, the king of Rome, and it was Capelle's idea to offer Germaine one last opportunity to redeem herself in the Emperor's eyes: he suggested that she write some eulogy concerning the blessed event: "One day [Capelle] came and proposed that I write something complimentary about the birth of the king of Rome," Germaine relates in her marvelous posthumously published book *Dix années d'exil.* "I replied, laughing, that I did not have one thought in mind about that subject, and that the most I could do was to wish him a good wet nurse."[239]

This impudent reply further incited the Emperor's rage. A few weeks later, after ordering Germaine back from an unauthorized excursion to Aix-les-Bains, Cappelle served notice that she would henceforth not be allowed to travel further than two leagues, in any direction, from Coppet. Having turned Germaine into a quasi-prisoner, he also ordered Schlegel to leave Coppet on the grounds that he was responsible for making Germaine "anti-French." That particular step in the Emperor's increasing repression of her liberty, and his officials' general pettiness, is also best narrated in Germaine's own words: "Truly touched by the French government's paternal solicitude towards me, I asked [Capelle] what M. Schlegel had ever done against France. The prefect proffered some literary opinions, and then handed me a pamphlet in which Schlegel, comparing Euripides's *Phaedra* to Racine's, had expressed a preference for Euripides's version."[240]

Schlegel left for Vienna with a manuscript of *De l'Allemagne,* removing it even further from Savary's reach. He eventually settled in Bern, which was to be his new home, except for frequent (and secret) stays at Coppet.

The Emperor's new tactic of isolating Germaine from her closest friends next affected Mathieu de Montmorency. Defying Capelle's orders, she had met Mathieu beyond the prescribed limit, at a Trappist convent near Fribourg where Schlegel joined then. As a result Mathieu was exiled from Paris and ordered to live outside of a radius of forty leagues from the capital. Germaine was alarmed: at that very minute Juliette was on her way to Coppet, and she feared the Emperor would dole out a similar punishment to her if she reached her destination. Auguste de Staël was sent to meet Juliette at her border and tried to convince her not to come to Coppet, and to visit with Germaine in some other, secret allocation instead. But Juliette insisted on continuing her journey, and at the end of August 1811, the two women, weeping with joy, were reunited. Within less than twenty-four hours of her arrival Juliette's nephew, a conservative French government official then stationed at Geneva, was so horrified by his aunt's disobedient conduct that he forcibly led her back to Paris. "Coppet is in mourning," Capelle reported to the Emperor. "So much the better. It will be a good lesson."[241] But a week later far worse news reached Germaine: to make sure that the two women could not meet again the government ordered Juliette to choose a domicile at a forty leagues' distance from Paris, and remain there until further notice.

The Emperor's new methods of persecuting Germaine were now clear. To prevent her from escaping to England via either America or Russia, the most probable routes of flight, he ordered her quarantined from her closest friends. Moreover, she was being more closely surveyed than ever. Police spies were posted throughout the village of Coppet. Cappelle bribed a few servants to report on every happening occurring at the château itself and bribed others to read and report on all her outgoing and ingoing mail. Germaine's definition of exile as "a tomb in which you can get mail" was all too painfully materializing, and she clearly sensed that the government's next step might be to incarcerate her. "I thus spent eight months in an indescribably [miserable] state," she wrote in *Dix années d'exil*, "constantly trying to boost my courage but seeing it diminish daily at the thought of eventual imprisonment."

Yet it was at this most tragic moment of Germaine's life, in her forty-fifth year, that the kind of man she had most desired throughout her life—one who loved her deeply—finally made his appearance.

Germaine first met Jean-Michel Rocca, known to all as Jean Rocca, in the winter of 1810–1811, at the house of mutual friends. His father, a counselor of state descended from a patrician Genevan family of Piedmontese origins, was a dour, taciturn Calvinist. His mother had died a few days after his birth. Describing the childhood he spent alone with his father, Rocca once wrote: "We were afraid to speak to each other, and lived side by side in a continuous silence which neither of us dared break."[242] Notwithstanding his unhappy, lonely childhood, Rocca developed into a splendid specimen of manhood. Tall, slender, handsome, beautifully built, with a thick black mustache and sideburns, he was a fervent sportsman, and a gifted hunter, swimmer, and rider; but he was also endowed with a poetic sensibility and a romantic yearning for the exotic and the adventurous. Napoleon's victorious campaigns having glorified the military life, he ran away from home at the age of seventeen to enlist in the French army. Rocca joined the 2nd Regiment of Hussars in Germany, probably fought in the battle of Iéna and was eventually promoted to second lieutenant. After a few years spent with the occupation forces in Germany and Holland, he was transferred to Spain.

In 1810, when a unit he was leading was ambushed, Rocca's left thigh was fractured by a bullet, an injury that forced him to walk with a crutch for the rest of his life. At the age of twenty-three he was put on permanent sick leave and returned to his family in the company of his beloved horse, Sultan, whose own war wounds had healed far better than his master's. Poorly educated, Rocca was at a dire loss about what direction to take in life now that he was unfit for military service. It is in that first year of his convalescence, at the home of his aunt Mme Argent-Picot, that Rocca met Germaine. The notorious lady, her stout frame magisterially draped in a large shawl, her turban surmounted by brilliant feathers, warmly addressed him, as he recalled it, with "a few words of pity" about his invalid condition, and before leaving casually asked him to attend the monthly concerts at her home. Fascinated by her sheer fame and by the brilliance of her conversation, of which he only understood a part, Rocca had been staring at her throughout the evening, transfixed. He had experienced love at first sight.

It is hard to explain why Rocca, who would have made an attractive husband for innumerable pretty young women, fell passionately in love with a stout, very plain matron twenty-seven years his senior, a woman "ravaged," as an earlier biographer puts it, by "passion, opium, and grief."[243] Was his motherless childhood at the heart of his infatuation with Germaine, or some chivalric sense which incited him to come to the help of a persecuted citizen?

Rocca was not gifted in the art of self-expression, so the nature of Germaine's spell on him will always remain mysterious. Whatever fueled his passion, it became totally obsessive. Beyond attending every concert and theatrical event given at her house, he appeared at all social gatherings that he knew she would attend. He was too shy to declare his passion to her directly, but he broadcast it to everyone else. "I shall love her so much," he boasted, "that she will end up by marrying me."[244] Aware that there was only one feat with which he could impress the world—ride his horse superbly—he appeared every day under Germaine's window on the steeply sloping Grand'Rue, even when it was perilously covered with ice, to perform some daring act of prowess with Sultan.

Meanwhile, Germaine, notwithstanding the debacle of *De l'Allemagne,* was continuing to put up a tranquil, stoic front to the Genevese, if only to deny them the pleasure of seeing her defeated. The suppression of the book had hurt her far more than she would allow anyone to know. Barante had been successfully excluded from her company by his father, who had obtained a position outside of France for him. To allay her solitude and depression she indulged, for the first time, in religious consolation by reading Fénelon and *The Imitation of Christ.* Only to Juliette Récamier did she reveal her true state of mind, and her puzzled reaction to John Rocca's amorous antics: "This new sentiment concerns a young man of twenty-three, handsome as the day. . . . But his mind is not at all cultivated and there is no future in the relationship. . . . I needed a diversion to bear [the suffering] I carry in the bottom of my heart. . . . His very noble character makes it safe, and as you know, a love which one inspires has the power, for a while, to console and distract."[245]

Though the fulfillment of Rocca's courtship did not seem that promising, there was one major factor in his favor: Constant was away for the time being, "playing at husband," as Germaine put it, "in a rather affected way."[246] (He had been visiting his father with Charlotte, hoping to retain his inheritance by having his wife accepted by his family.) So after a few months of Rocca paying court, Germaine was writing Juliette that she no longer suffered from those "crises of despair"[247] that had earlier tormented her. All of Genevese society noticed there was a new serenity in her demeanor, and a new young man perpetually at her side. At one particular dinner party to which both had been invited, a guest noticed that Rocca was amusing himself by making Sultan go down a dangerous ramp at a canter. Germaine fainted upon hearing this and upon recovering ordered a search for her lover. After he'd reappeared and apologized there followed a scene of tearful reproaches. A short while afterward, the comedy was repeated at the dinner table, when the hostess asked Rocca to carve the roast. Upon his taking up the carving knife, so their hostess tells it,

"Madame de Staël gave a piercing scream, cried to us to disarm him so that he would not kill himself, and fainted all over again."[248]

Anecdotes about Germaine have always tended to be embellished, but such hysterical episodes were not infrequent with her. She had had hallucinations since childhood—yet another symptom of bipolar disorder—and over the years her use of opium had greatly increased similar occurrences. Scenes such as these, however, were telling society that Madame de Staël and Rocca were now a "couple" in every sense of the word. At another social event, when, in apology for Rocca having uttered an inanity, Germaine whispered to her hostess, "Ah! Speech is not his language!"[249] there was little doubt concerning the nature of their relationship.

Germaine returned to Coppet in early spring, Rocca in tow. Barante, complaining of the coldness of her letters, hinted that he knew of the "sentimental experiments" she was dabbling with in Geneva. Chamiso, who'd been waiting for her at Coppet, packed up his guitar and left in disgust. No one was more dismayed than Schlegel by Germaine's "frivolous infatuation."[250] In revenge, he nicknamed his new rival Caliban, a name that stayed with Rocca for the rest of his life. The only inhabitants of Coppet not vexed by Rocca's arrival were Germaine's children, who immediately accepted him as an adopted older brother. Germaine had always proclaimed that her life's goal was to be loved in just this manner—with total, passionate devotion. Yet the relationship troubled her.

What kind of impression would Rocca make in Vienna, Paris, or London? Was he perhaps *insortable*? She set about to educate him, to have him read books, to write about his war experiences in Spain. The pupil worked hard and made progress, but he clearly could never give her the intellectual satisfaction of a Constant or a Schlegel. She loved him sincerely, and if he had tried to abandon her, she might have fallen passionately in love with him. So here was the irony: She had found just the kind of love she'd sought all her life, but not the happiness she'd hoped for in such a love.

Meanwhile Rocca, while athletically indulging his lust for Germaine, was telling her that she must marry him; he even insisted that she bear him a child, a "Little Us." Rocca was as obstinate as he was ardent. And on May 1811, in the sole presence of a Protestant pastor and Fanny Randall, Germaine and John Rocca made vows to marry "as soon as circumstances permitted." This bizarre half-marriage, half-engagement pledge was maintained in absolute secrecy—even Germaine's children never knew about it. Rocca proved so possessive that in the next month there were two occasions when Germaine had to stop him from forcing Benjamin into a duel. Another swain had to be dismissed—Barante. This admirer, who seems to have been as readily intoxicated as Germaine by the rhetoric of love, reacted woefully. "Why have I ever known you, Corinne? Why have I lived with you that exalted, intoxicating life ... after having tasted of the food and drink of the gods, what burning regrets hark back to the lost pleasures!"[251] He took advantage of his freedom soon enough: two months later he was engaged to be married to a Mademoiselle d'Houdenot, a young woman Germaine knew well and who may have served as a model for the fictional Lucile Edgermond, half-sister of Germaine's Corinne.

Whatever passion was encompassing her, Germaine continued to feel like a prisoner, isolated from most of her intimates. Her little court was reduced to Rocca and her children. "I feel as if I were on guard duty over my tomb," she would write Hochet in the following months.[252] "I spend whole hours familiarizing myself with the idea of death,"[253] she wrote Juliette Récamier. Curiously, these morbid musings were motivated by the knowledge of her pregnancy. Rocca ever at her side, Germaine, looking sallow, haggard, deformed, managed to hide her growing hulk under voluminous skirts and shawls; she was only too aware of the ridicule she might suffer if it became known that she'd been impregnated at the age of forty-five by a man young enough to be her son, and she spent the last months of her pregnancy ingeniously hiding her condition. Intimates and closest friends, even Schlegel and her children, were led to think that she was suffering from an attack of dropsy.

When Germaine needed it, she was capable of remarkable self-control. It is hard to believe the success of her deceitfulness, but the following fact must be taken at face value, since no one in her family ever denied it: On April 7, at Coppet, in the sole company of her personal physician and of Miss Randall, Germaine gave birth to a boy without the rest of her family—Albert, Albertine, and Schlegel—

knowing anything about it. After a few days spent with his parents, the infant was taken by a doctor friend and Miss Randall to a village near the town of None, where he was baptized by a Protestant clergyman, Pastor Gleyre, as "Louis Alphonse, son of Henriette, née Preston, and of Theodore Giles, of Boston" (these parents' names were purely fictional). The infant remained in the care of the pastor and his wife, and Germaine did not see him again for another two years.

All this time Germaine was being watched more carefully than ever by Capelle, the spy assigned to her by the Emperor. Capelle, shrewd enough to have guessed the cause of her recent corpulence, learned that she had liquidated a large part of her fortune and was carrying it on her in cash. He knew that she would soon try to escape Switzerland, and he was right, but not quite vigilant enough. In the early afternoon of May 23, after ordering that night's dinner, Germaine and Albertine climbed into an open carriage—the kind used for brief afternoon drives—carrying no visible baggage other than their fans. They were not to see Coppet again for another fourteen months. Soon changing to a series of more substantial vehicles, they went on to visit Austria, Russia, Sweden, and England before returning home. Notwithstanding all his precautions, M. Capelle only discovered Germaine's absence ten days after she had left. By that time she had crossed into Austria.

Germaine met Schlegel in a village near Bern and asked him to arrange visas for herself and for her family for Austria, and, eventually, for Russia. Schlegel drew the line at the notion of Rocca's company, so she had to temporarily leave him behind (Schlegel ultimately softened toward Rocca, and the latter rejoined the party in Salzburg). Within the next weeks Uginet, her factotum, arrived with her baggage, and Germaine reached Vienna in early June. She followed Auguste's advice to not be seen in the company of Rocca, and he was assigned to a small boarding house, respectably distant from Germaine's party, from which he visited his mistress after dark. Her social life was minimal—apart from a few old friends. Her Viennese acquaintances feared to compromise themselves by being seen with such a militant leader of the anti-Bonapartist faction. She next spent anxious weeks waiting for her Russian passports, and when Schlegel arrived with them, her flight continued. Soon she crossed into Russia, swearing never again "to set foot in any country which was in any way subject to Emperor Napoleon." Since most of western Europe was now suffering that plight, her immense enthusiasm for Russia was in part based on the fact that she looked on it as a land of liberty.

On May 9, 1812, two weeks after Germaine's flight from Coppet, Napoleon, meeting in Dresden with several heads of state, ordered his special envoy, the Comte de Narbonne (who had had a smashing diplomatic career since his tryst with Germaine) to carry his ultimatum to Tsar Alexander I of Russia. "Time and space are [in my favor],"[254] the Tsar told Narbonne, pointing to the map of Russia, insisting that he would defend the most remote corners of his empire rather than consent to the dishonorable peace the French Emperor was trying to impose on him. Narbonne brought the news back to Napoleon. At the end of May the Emperor ordered a half million men to gather in Poland, and in the latter part of June they began to cross into Russia.

Napoleon's invasion of Russia occurred a fortnight before Germaine entered it. St. Petersburg being her ultimate destination, she had to take complex detours to avoid the Emperor's armies, voyaging through Kiev, Orel, Moscow, and Novgorod to reach Peter's city. And her readers should be grateful that these circumventions greatly lengthened her stay, for her pages on Russia, in *Dix années d'exil,* offer some of the finest prose she ever wrote. There was something about the particulars of Russian architecture and landscape, and the complexity of the Russian temperament (she did not seem to realize, or to acknowledge, how similar it was to hers) that she found deeply inspirational. She dwelt at length on the specific characteristics of the Slavic ethos. "It is built into the character of this people to not fear fatigue or any form of physical suffering. There is patience in this country... gaiety and melancholy. One witnesses the most striking contrasts in all matters of things, which presages greatness because usually only superior beings are gifted with opposite qualities."[255]

She immediately grasped the impetuous prodigality of the national character: "The colossal fortunes of the great Russian nobles are used... to create great festivities modeled on *A Thousand and One Nights,* and these fortunes are very often lost by the unleashed passions of those who possess them."[256] About the Russian upper classes she wrote that they were "both impetuous and reserved, more capable of passion than of friendship, more proud than delicate, more religious than virtuous . . . and so violent in their desires that nothing will stop them from satisfying them"—traits that she traced back to the Russians' unique blend of "European civilization and Asiatic character."[257] For if there is one theme Germaine dwelt on most obsessively in her chapters on Russia, it is the "Asiatic" or "Oriental" nature of the Slavic temperament. Russians were Oriental in the way they "showed hospitality to strangers, lavished presents on them and often neglected the comfort of their own lives."[258] She mentions one grand seigneur, M. Narychkine, who was deeply bored if there were only twenty persons staying with him in his country dacha.[259] She writes about a Count Stroganoff whose hospitality was so excessive that "he often did not know more than half of the persons who dined at his house . . . but this luxury of hospitality pleased him, being another form of munificence."[260]

Equally receptive to the physical beauty of Russian landscape, and of its architecture, she was particularly taken with the sheer emptiness of Russia's steppes, and by the illusional magnificence of its churches: traveling through the vast stretches of uninhabited Russia—it took her a fortnight to journey by coach from Kiev to Moscow—she found it like "a country recently deserted by its nation, so few houses can one see, so little noise is there to hear."[261] "When the evening sun bestows its rays upon the brilliant domes of its churches, one feels an illumination has been temporarily created in honor of a festive occasion."[262]

Although the phrases "Kindness and dignity" and "Noble simplicity" often recur in her descriptions of the Russian aristocracy, Germaine was critical of Russians' intellectual life: "The national character is too passionate to enjoy any form of abstract thought . . . the charm of Russian society does not consist in conversation, but in the elegance of its lifestyle. . . . One enjoys oneself well enough in this amiable and dazzling atmosphere, but in the long run there is nothing to learn from it, one does not develop one's intellectual faculties, and the men who spend their time in it do not acquire any inclinations for serious issues."[263] She also found them inconstant in their loves: "A certain disorderliness of their imagination doesn't permit them to find any happiness in duration . . . in these fantastical and vehement natures, love is a festivity or a delirium rather than a deep and measured devotion."[264] She was very moved, however, by the intensely religious character of the population at large: "Russians seldom pass in front of a church without doing the sign of the cross, and their faith in the visible images of their religion is very touching. They carry into their churches that taste for luxury which they inherit from Asia: One only sees in them ornaments of gold, silver and rubies."[265] She was struck by the lack of a bourgeoisie in Russia, which she astutely predicted was on the verge of arising. And she made a curious comment on the nobility's attitude toward the Tsar's autocracy. "Used to being the absolute masters of their own serfs, they wish their monarch to be all-powerful to maintain the hierarchy of despotism."[266] Civilization as Western Europeans know it, she found, had not yet penetrated into Russia, not even into its own nobility. "Some have surface resemblances to the French, others to Germans, others to the British, but all are deeply Russian, and this is what makes for their power and their originality, love of motherland being, after the love of God, the most beautiful emotion men can experience."[267]

It should be noted that Germaine was visiting Russia during the very month Napoleon was attacking it, a few weeks before the burning of Moscow, and that she was surrounded by a citizenry of vehement anti-Bonapartists, feeling "immense pleasure to hear everyone expressing the sentiments I'd so often stifled in my own soul."[268] (Having compared Napoleon in *De l'Allemagne* to Attila, in *Dix années d'exil* she refers to him as "an African tyrant."[269]) She may well have been at her most prophetic when she wrote, fifteen and fifty years, respectively, before the appearance of Pushkin's and Tolstoy's masterpieces, about the state of Russian literature. "Genius will come to them in the fine arts, and particularly in literature, when they will have found a way of funneling their deepest nature into language as well as they have into their actions."[270]

One wonders how Germaine would have reacted to the observation that her own personality was intensely akin to the national character she was describing. Those similarities are at their most striking when she writes about

Russians being both "tyrannical and self-sacrificing," when she states that one of their great failings is a self-destructive capacity for boredom, that "fury and ruse" fill them when they go about accomplishing what they have resolved, that the impetuous violence of Russian desire was "capable of blowing up a city."[271] In sum, the Russian character, like Germaine's, was extreme, savagely impulsive, prodigal to a fault. That may be why the Russians took to Germaine as instinctually and enthusiastically as she took to them. In Moscow, just before the great fire that he is said to have instigated, she dined at the estate of Governor Rostopchin, and many other Moscovites—it was late June—flocked back to the city from their dachas to see the famous French woman. Their enthusiasm was not unanimous: the poet Alexander Pushkin quotes one lady of society who described Germaine as "a fat woman of fifty dressed inappropriately for her years. . . . Her speeches [were] too long and her sleeves [were] too short."[272]

Germaine's remarks on the frivolity of Moscow conversation predates by a few decades Tolstoy's pastiche of that society. She far preferred St. Petersburg, which teemed with Western ideas and intellectual vitality. Social life there continued unchanged as Napoleon approached Moscow. She had two long têtes-a-têtes with the highly enlightened, progressive Emperor Alexander I and, addressing him with startling forthrightness, criticized him for not taking stronger measures against serfdom (he meekly replied that he was taking measures to "ameliorate the plight of the peasantry.") She read from *De l'Allemagne* at the salon of Count Orlov and discussed politics with the British Ambassador, at the Foreign Ministry. She was ill at ease with the Russian aristocracy's virulently anti-French opinions. A quandary was confronting her that would continue to plague her for the next two years. How to separate France's cause from Napoleon's? How to simultaneously wish for France's victory and Napoleon's defeat? Before she set off for Sweden the Tsar asked her to wield her influence over General Bernadotte, Sweden's Crown Prince, and persuade him to join the Allied Coalition against the French Emperor. The Tsar's hidden agenda was to have Russia lead a European coalition against Napoleon, to have him overthrown, and to see the establishment of a liberal constitutional monarchy in France with Prince Bernadotte as king. Germaine set about working for these goals, which she more or less shared. It is certain that no person did more than she to promote Sweden's participation in the war against Bonaparte, and that Sweden played a crucial role in the French Emperor's defeat.

Germaine's original purpose, in setting forth for Sweden, was to find good positions for her sons. Arriving there with her retinue—Albertine, Albert, Schlegel, and Rocca—she was received by Crown Prince Bernadotte like an old friend, and her wishes concerning her sons were granted. Albert received a commission in the Hussars of the Royal Guards; his older brother, Auguste, who arrived a few weeks late because he had fallen in love, to his mother's despair, with Juliette Récamier, was promised a position as aide-de-camp; and Schlegel was made the Crown Prince's private secretary. But an equally important goal of this trip to Stockholm was to draw Bernadotte into the Alliance against the French Emperor, since he was the only man, in Germaine's opinion, who could "stem Napoleon's tide."[273] In her four-room apartment facing the opera house, she received the entire diplomatic corps, with the exception of the French ambassador. By then Napoleon, defeated by the Russians' valor and cunning, was rushing back to Paris, having deliberately abandoned twenty-thousand wounded French men on Russian soil. Back in Paris, he used every possible public relations tactic that came into his head to keep the French nation from realizing the extent of his defeat. By mid-March, Sweden and England, with much lobbying on the part of Germaine, had concluded a treaty whereby Bernadotte promised to join the Allied coalition against Napoleon, and to land thirty thousand men in French-occupied Pomerania that spring. King Frederick William of Prussia followed Sweden's example a few weeks later. Bernadotte's army kept Napoleon at bay and forced him to agree to a cease-fire; it also gave the European Coalition time to recover from their losses and to convince Austria to join them. Once the war resumed in July, Napoleon's situation had become hopeless. "A Frenchman held the destiny of France in his hands," the deposed Emperor wrote during his last years at Saint Helena. "[Bernadotte] was one of the principal direct causes of our misfortune."[274]

Germaine's role in these diplomatic cabals led one wit—the Austrian army officer Baron de Mansert—to make the following remark: there were "three independent powers left in the world—Britain, Russia, and Mme de Staël."[275] But during her stay in Sweden Germaine did not enjoy her triumph. The shortage of sun and the frivolous vacuity of Swedish high society depressed her deeply. Bernadotte's absence, and Schlegel's, created a great emptiness. Sweden's elite, not unlike Vienna's, was both awed by her and eager to criticize her. One witness at a ball described her thus:

"The door was thrown open, and she entered. . . . Alas, an illusion crumbled. There was nothing of a Corinne or Delphine about her. She was a corpulent person, very thick set, without any gracefulness in her movements. She always kept her head thrown back and never seemed to stop looking at the ceiling with her lively and mobile eyes; because of this attitude, her mouth was always half open, even when she was not talking, which happened rarely."[276]

And then there were always complaints about the flamboyant clothes, the "voluminous, multi-colored turban."[277] As for Albertine, a great beauty who combined a very liberated manner with considerable dignity of deportment, she was found to be "the most lively, natural and free person," even though she was "draped rather than dressed."[278] Each time her draperies slipped from her shoulders, Rocca assumed his paternal role and decorously placed them back again.

After six months spent in Stockholm, in the last days of May 1813, Germaine sailed to England with Rocca, Auguste, and Albertine, hoping to meet Constant there. For the past two years, he had been suffering through his very unhappy marriage, gambling more disastrously than ever, and often deploring Germaine's absence from his life. "Good letter from Mme de Staël," his journal entries for the spring of that year run. "Confounded marriage, shall I ever get out of it? ... More serious quarrel than ever with Charlotte. I believe that [fundamentally] we are through with each other." "Germaine's voyage is all over the papers." "Direct news from the traveler, God be praised! How I regret Mme de Staël ... I regret Mme de Staël more than ever."[279] However gratefully Germaine appreciated Rocca's love, his jealousy and the exclusivity of his passion exasperated her; and the longings expressed in Constant's diary are paralleled in her own letters to him. "What is to become of me in my spiritual solitude?" she asks him. "Whom can I talk to? ... My father, you and Mathieu," she adds, "have a place in my heart now closed forever ... there I live and die."[280]

That missive was written on the eve of her departure to England. When she arrived at Lord Landsdowne's, one of the first Londoners to hold a reception in her honor, guests of both genders climbed on chairs to see her. How could they not welcome the only Continental power to have combated Napoleon as passionately as they had? The British publisher John Murray bought the rights to publish her *De l'Allemagne* for 1,500 guineas, a good sum for those times. It sold out in three days and made her all the more the social star of that London season (she had sent Rocca away to Bath, both for reasons of social propriety and for his ill health—he had recently been diagnosed with tuberculosis). Yet one sorrowful incident marred the pleasures she enjoyed in Great Britain: she had not been there for six weeks when she learned that her son Albert had been killed.

Twenty-year-old Albert had always been a wild, hot-headed youth (Schlegel had referred to him as "Hotspur," and his mother nicknamed him "Lovelace"). And his recent military assignment to Hamburg, where he kept company with Cossack regiments, made his behavior all the more frenetic. He drank, gambled, and wenched with such abandon that Bernadotte, who felt responsible for his friend's son, exiled him for a week to an island. The punishment did not chasten Albert. Soon after his release he picked a quarrel with a Russian officer during a bout of gambling, and a duel was scheduled. The following day Albert was killed by one thrust of the Russian's sword. Germaine's sorrow was not that evident—there were occasions upon which she was able totally to control herself and grieve silently, and this was one of them. The death of Narbonne, later that year, seems to have affected her almost as much as their son's.

After reporting that her book had been "madly successful," she wrote to Schlegel that death seemed to haunt her more than ever. "Life hurts me, and I can think of no remedy except seeing you. I always felt that my father intended you to close my eyes."[281] Germaine was indeed more alone than ever. Constant, mostly from inertia, did not reply to her requests to join her in London. Schlegel was totally absorbed by his post as Bernadotte's aide-de-camp. His principal communications concerned Albert's numerous unpaid bills. At one point Germaine simply refused to pay them, writing Schlegel, "We must think of [our own future] and of those of our children who have been sensible and obedient."[282] To secure a good marriage for Albertine now seemed to absorb her more than her love life, or the fate of the world. But she kept this particular anxiety to herself, and the old fire still shone in her eyes and her conversation. "She interrupted Whitbread," Byron reminisced in 1821 about Germaine's stay in London, "she declaimed to Lord Liverpool, she harangued, she lectured, she preached English politics to the first of our English Whig politicians the day after her arrival in England. . . . The Sovereign himself . . . was not exempt from this flow of eloquence."[283]

Germaine and Byron saw each other many times during the winter of 1813–1814, and though at first he was sharp-tongued toward her his tone soon changed to one of respect and playful affection. "She interrupted me every moment," he told Lady Blessington, "by gesticulating, exclaiming *'Quelle idée! Mon Dieu! Ecoutez donc! Vous m'impatientez!'*"[284] Germaine enjoyed equally warm relations with the great abolitionist William Wilberforce, who inspired her to devote much time, in her last years, to antislavery causes. And from October to Christmas of 1813 she spent a large share of her time as a guest in England's greatest country houses—the Marquess of Salisbury's, the Duchess of Devonshire's. Most of us would not weary so fast when enjoying some of England's finest architecture, and its grandest hosts. But boredom was Germaine's most plaguing psychic ailment. "What I feel above all is boredom," she wrote Rocca, whom she still kept in exile at Bath, having ordered him to learn English there, and to get into the habit of reading more books. In January Rocca settled in London to be nearer her. But he had his burdensome side, tending to be overly casual, and was not allowed to present himself at her apartment without being in formal dress, with hat and cane in hand. His politics—like many a former army man, he was still an unreconstructed Bonapartist—also compromised her. "Please do be more careful," she scolded him, "you will ruin me."[285] Moreover, Rocca was highly possessive and wildly jealous. He utterly failed to understand why Germaine, if she truly loved him, had to seek the company of others round the clock, and still called for Constant and Schlegel to be at her side.

In sum, toward the end of her stay in London Germaine seemed at loose ends. She spoke of traveling to Greece, to Ireland, back to Germany. The political situation made her confusion even worse. After Napoleon's catastrophic defeat at Leipzig, the Allies began to pour into France. Germaine suddenly felt a great surge of guilt: She realized she had been fraternizing with her country's enemies. From now on she had to make everyone understand that Napoleon's cause had to be detached from that of the French nation. It was clear that she was looked on as a true power when an emissary of the Comte de Provence, Louis XVI's younger brother and the future Louis XVIII, called on her; Provence had been exiled in England since the Revolution, and his emissary invited her to "lend her pen," as he put it, to his restoration. Germaine, who initially had been adamantly against the return of the

Bourbons, pretended she had no influence whatsoever. But over the following weeks she began to accept the probability of the Bourbons' return to power. "The Duc de Berry (Louis XVIII's nephew) has come to see me," she wrote Benjamin. "If they return, we must submit rather than risk more troubles, and I am on reasonable terms with the Bourbons."[286] She finally went to call on the future Louis XVIII to offer him her support.

As for Constant, ever the opportunist, he had seen a new political possibility: he would make a career on Bernadotte's coattails. Even Schlegel had the same purpose in mind; for once, Constant and Schlegel had a common cause and, united by their loathing for Napoleon, held a series of long meetings together. Encouraged by Schlegel, Constant wrote a pamphlet that aimed to help the Allies in their struggle against Napoleon—*On the Spirit of Conquest and on Usurpation*. (It would become such a classic of French polemical writing that it was even reprinted several times during World War II). He sent it on to Germaine, who was critical of it because she was so upset about the Allies' invasion of Paris. "One must not speak ill of the French . . . when the Russians are at Langres," she wrote him. "May God banish me from France rather than let me return with the help of foreigners! . . . Do you really want the Cossacks in the Rue Racine?"[287]

She wrote to a member of the British cabinet, using the same reasoning: "I want Bonaparte to be victorious and to be killed in battle."[288] Bernadotte, meanwhile, realizing that his opportunity to gain the French throne was lost, went home to Sweden incognito, greatly disappointing Constant and Schlegel. And who was the man who single-handedly persuaded Tsar Alexander and the French Senate to proclaim Napoleon's deposition and the restoration of King Louis XVIII? No one other than Talleyrand. Constant, seeing yet another opportunity, wrote Talleyrand a note and rushed to Paris to meet him. He found the über-diplomat well disposed toward him. "Let us help the good cause and let us help ourselves,"[289] Constant wrote in his diary with typical cynicism.

Germaine was able to go home to Paris freely for the first time in twelve years, but she was hardly joyful about it. "What are you congratulating me on, pray—that I am in despair?"[290] she answered a friend who was welcoming her back to the capital. But in the next weeks she made her peace—dispassionately, as her attitude now tended to be—with the prospect of a Bourbon Restoration. Upon his first meeting with Germaine in two years Constant noted that she was thin and pale, and that she was "utterly changed." He found her "distracted . . . almost arid, thinking only of herself . . . caring about nothing, even [for] her daughter only from duty, and not at all for me."[291]

Chapter 15

The Last Salons

Only Constant, who knew Germaine as did no one else, perceived that she was "utterly changed." To the rest of the world she seemed the same. She reopened her first Paris salon in twelve years, and a brilliant one it was. Tsar Alexander, Wellington, Bernadotte, Lafayette, Talleyrand, and Fouché attended her dinners, her teas, her receptions. (The last two defrocked ecclesiastics, having served the Revolution, the Directory, the Consulate, and the Empire, were now the *éminences grises* of Louis XVIII's regime.) She continued to retain her consistently centrist political views, and also her bellicose, combative tone. She had promised her allegiance to a Bourbon restoration on the condition that it be accompanied by a liberal constitution. And when Louis XVIII, under the influence of Tsar Alexander, set forth his constitution—referred to as the Charter of 1814—she was not satisfied with it. In her opinion it did not express enough enthusiasm for the Revolution, it was not truly bicameral, and it did not enough fulfill the French people's thousand-year struggle for freedom.

To defend the Revolution as the turning point in that struggle for liberty, she began to write the book that would become the principal inspirational tract for French liberals for decades to come: her *Considérations sur la Révolution française*. Having been strongly influenced by John Wilberforce's book against slavery, for whose French edition she wrote the preface, she also focused her energies on the rights of Negroes and published a pamphlet that urged every government to abolish the ebony trade. England was now her second home, and Wellington her greatest hero. Mostly as a favor to Juliette Récamier, she also secretly conspired to maintain Joachim Murat on the throne of Naples. These intrigues became known by the new French sovereign, Louis XVIII, who eventually sent her a laconic message, a put-down rather than a threat, that stated: "We attach so little importance to anything you do, say or write that the government [will not] allow anyone to hinder you in any way in your projects and mysteries."[292] In sum, she resumed indulging in her principal passion—politicking. "I detest talking about politics," her friend the Duke of Wellington said to her one day. "But talking politics is my whole life,"[293] she blurted out.

Behind this abidingly bold facade, her very closest friends began to notice the changes in her. Somewhere between Stockholm and her return to Paris, the old Germaine de Staël had died. Her sallow complexion, her loss of weight and her lack of energy signaled alarming changes in her health. Her attitude to friends was even more striking. It had always been in her character to be stridently demanding. She now seemed downright indifferent, although she criticized her friends more sharply than ever, breaking with Mathieu de Montmorency, for instance, because of his extreme pro-Royalist views. Her relationship with the two men she had known and loved the longest, Constant and Prosper de Barante, had become, as Constant put it, utterly "dry." Her lifelong searches for passion and happiness having ceased, the only person who mattered to her now was Rocca. So there they were, a bizarre and pathetic couple, a woman of forty-eight, a limping, perpetually coughing man of twenty-six, each weakening in health, each terrified of outliving the other.

Germaine's other principal preoccupation, after her return to Paris, was to find a suitable husband for her daughter. However beautiful she was, Albertine, forthright, rather haughty, highly intelligent, was thought to be too much of a bluestocking, some Parisians thought, to be easily marriageable. Moreover, a number of eligible young men might have been terrified to have Mme de Staël as a mother-in-law. Whatever Albertine's winsomeness and drawbacks, she would not have a suitable dowry if the government did not return the two million francs still owed her mother. Upon returning to Paris after Napoleon's abdication, Germaine had instantly begun to harass Louis XVIII's regime about this debt. The problem became all the more urgent when a fine candidate for Albertine's hand came to the fore, Duc Victor de Broglie, an intelligent, highly liberal, sensitive young man with no money but impeccable political credentials: his father, a pro-Revolutionary aristocrat, had been guillotined during the reign of Terror. His mother had been one of the countless aristocrats saved by Germaine's Scarlet Pimpernel ventures. The young Duke was of small but elegant stature, a man of perfect courtesy notwithstanding his rather dry, solemn manner. Broglie's appearance made Germaine's financial concerns all the more pressing.

Then the summer came, and Germaine returned to Coppet. Her lover was terribly ill, and her financial worries made her more of an insomniac than ever. What kept her going was simply a sense of duty toward her family and to Rocca. "I must keep on rowing," she wrote her cousin that year, "not until I reach port [by which she meant, in the context of the letter, happiness] but until I reach my grave."[294] Summer life at Coppet resumed its habitual schedule. Schlegel unpacked his bags in his book-lined "blue room"; Bonstetten, Sismondi, and Mrs. Randall returned to their usual quarters. There was the typical stream of visitors, but since Germaine had just about ceased sleeping at night she had plenty of time to continue her works in progress: *Dix années d'exil,* and *Considérations.*

It was during those months at Coppet that Germaine came to the rescue of the man who had ruined her life for the previous decade and a half, displaying again her magnanimity and her utter lack of vindictiveness. One of her guests having informed her that there was a plot to assassinate Napoleon at Elba, Germaine rushed to the nearby château where the Emperor's brother, Joseph, lived and offered to go to Elba herself to prevent the attack on the former Emperor. A less-visible messenger was sent out to Elba, but Napoleon was informed of Germaine's gesture and conveyed his gratitude.

While at Coppet Germaine continued to be plagued by her financial problems—even though she was trying to raise a dowry for their own daughter, Constant disdainfully refused to return her the 80,000 francs she had loaned him years ago, pleading that he had promised to bequeath the money in his will. But it was not only Albertine's dowry that concerned her: she wished to legitimize her bonds with Rocca and the existence of "Little Us." Rocca and Germaine paid their son a furtive visit that year—they found him eerily quiet and timid, with a head a bit too large for his size. Whether he had suffered an injury, or had been raised in too great isolation, he would be analyzed, in contemporary terms, as being a backward, perhaps autistic, child. But his parents did not seem to be aware of this, and although Germaine felt duty rather than fondness for the boy, Rocca adored him, and the visits to his son were the highlights of his year.

The summer was marked by one major emotional upheaval—Constant's sudden infatuation for Juliette Récamier, whom he had observed for over twelve years without a flutter of passion. Juliette, responding as usual with her quixotic blend of coquettishness and frigidity, led him to the verge of a breakdown. He spent whole days and nights in crying fits and found his main solace in disastrous bouts of gambling. One day, longing to unburden his heart, he called on seventeen-year-old Albertine and confided his despair to her. Albertine, a calm and precociously wise girl, reported his confession fully to her mother. Some days later, Benjamin made his confession to Germaine herself. Germaine pretended to respond sympathetically. He must make the semblance of courting another woman, she said, that was the only way to make headway with such a coquette. But that was playacting: under her calm exterior she seethed with fury: The gambling incited by Benjamin's new passion had led him to fall into deeper debt than ever, with little chance of ever paying back his debt to Germaine. She retaliated with an action totally atypical of her: she spoke ill of Juliette to Constant, and of Constant to Juliette, and after a few months Constant's infatuation for the seducer ended as suddenly as it had begun.

On March 1, 1815, the French citizenry was confronted with the greatest political surprise of the decade: Napoleon had landed in Toulon and was on his way back to Paris, unopposed, his army gathering strength town by town as his old soldiers joined his initially ragged band. Upon hearing of the landing, Louis XVIII fled to Belgium. A few days later, Germaine sped back to Coppet with Rocca, Schlegel, and Albertine, feeling, as she wrote in her *Considérations,* "as if the earth was about to open up under my feet."[295] As for Constant, the master of opportunism, his behavior became more fickle than ever. Earlier that year he had written two fervently pro-Bourbon articles for the *Journal des Débats,* France's most influential political periodical, which were filled with furious invectives against the Corsican. But after Napoleon had made his triumphant reentry into the Tuileries, Constant was approached by Fouché, and then by Napoleon himself, to lend support to the Emperor.

Barely a month after his invectives against Napoleon, Constant published a fervently pro-Bonapartist essay in another publication, the *Journal de Paris*. The following week, Constant had several one-on-one meetings with the Emperor. Within a few days, he was nominated to the Conseil d'Etat, Napoleon's version of a cabinet, and asked to write a new constitution for France. He accepted. This charter for Napoleon's One Hundred Day Empire would go down in history as "La Benjamine."

During his hundred days' rule, Napoleon had extended an olive branch to Germaine as well as to Constant. But she did not accept it. Her continued loathing of the Emperor, and her contempt for Constant's cynicism, had led her to part company with many of her intimates: Sismondi, Lafayette, her own son Auguste, the latter of whom was graciously received by the Emperor, all had supported Constant. The only note of opportunism she showed the Emperor was the following: "If he [Napoleon] accepts the liquidation [of the debt] he may be sure that my gratitude will prevent me from writing or doing anything detrimental to him."[296] Bonaparte, who had barely a cent to his name, preferred to continue baiting her with the money, in hopes that she would "lend her pen" in supporting him—support she refused to give. When Napoleon invited her to Paris to celebrate the new Constitution he was offering France, she replied: "He got along well enough without me or a Constitution for twelve years, and even now, he doesn't like either of us any more than the other."[297] Inevitably, the day after Constant's nomination to the Conseil d'Etat, Germaine wrote him a letter accusing him of selling himself to the Emperor, and repeating her plea for him to repay his debt. He flatly refused. She wrote him again, threatening to sue him. He resorted vilely to blackmail: He had kept all her letters, he warned, and if she sued him, he would make them public. "I will crush her,"[298] he wrote in his diary. "This last stroke is worthy of you, really worthy of you," Germaine replied. "To threaten a woman with intimate letters that would compromise her and her family, so as not to pay her the money he owes her, this is a device Monsieur de Sade has overlooked. . . . " In ending, she added: "Money alone determines your entire life, political as well as private."[299]

She could not keep from continuing to be involved in politics. She struck up a friendship with the Duc d'Orléans, a nephew of Louis XVI who like most of his family had sought exile in England, and would come to the throne fourteen years later as Louis-Philippe. Germaine preferred him to the passive, indolent Louis XVIII, and toward the end of the Hundred Days, when Napoleon seemed doomed, she tried to stir up enthusiasm for him to succeed the Emperor. She sent Broglie and Auguste to offer him her support and wrote him to say he was "the hand God had chosen to carry out His designs."[300] The Duc d'Orléans' reply, written in English, which he wrote far better than French, was courteous but negative concerning what he referred to as her "flattering dream."[301] One must remember, however, that when he came to the throne thirteen years after Germaine's death, he was uniquely empowered by Germaine's friends and political heirs—Broglie, Guizot, Barante, and her general milieu of centrist liberals.

When the Emperor was finally routed at Waterloo, Constant wrote dryly in his diary: "A debacle, it seems. God's will be done."[302] As Napoleon fled to La Rochelle to take ship for his final home—the desolate South Atlantic island of Saint Helena—Louis XVIII's government was back in place. Within days Constant succeeded in having his name deleted from the list of exiles that the restored Bourbon government had compiled and began to work on an essay that would exonerate his conduct during the Hundred Days.

It could not have been easy for Germaine in May 1816, when Constant, having "emerged from the delirium"[303] of his love for Juliette, finally published his novel *Adolphe:* Readers throughout Europe identified its heroine with Mme de Staël. She remained—or pretended to remain—unperturbed by this association. Its heroine, Ellénore, was based on Mrs. Lindsay, she said, not at all on her. Shortly after *Adolphe* was published she returned from Italy to Coppet with Albertine and her son-in-law, Victor de Broglie, who had just been married in Pisa (the debt owed Germaine by the French government for nearly three decades had at last been repaid earlier that year).

That last summer in Coppet—1816—was like the last act of a great opera. The hostess surpassed herself in entertaining her guests, for she provided them with the most talked-about man in Europe, Lord Byron. Byron, who would describe Mme de Staël as "the first female writer of this, or perhaps any age,"[304] lived that summer across the lake from Coppet, finishing the Third Canto of his *Childe Harold*. Outcast by all members of Genevan society except Germaine's circle, he created high drama when he first appeared at her house: Upon the majordomo announcing his name as he walked into Germaine's living room, one of the female guests fell to the floor in a dead faint and had to be carried out. The other guests, Byron recollected, "had come to stare at me as at some outlandish beast in a raree show."[305] In later years Byron would recall Germaine, who treated him with motherly solicitude, as "a very kind" woman; he was also very fond of Rocca, whom he referred to as "Monsieur l'amant." They had their arguments. Byron once told Germaine that Constant's *Adolphe,* which he much admired, had more morality than any novel she had written, and that "it ought always be given to every young woman who had read *Corinne,* as an antidote." Upon which, Byron wrote, "Mme de Staël came down upon me like an avalanche, sweeping everything before her, with that eloquence that always overwhelmed, but never convinced."[306]

During that last summer at Coppet, which Stendhal would refer to decades later as "The Estates General of Europe," most every European language could be heard, though English predominated (Lord Landsdowne and a score of British dukes set the tone). The numerous guests were squeezed uncomfortably at the dinner table, which was far too small to accommodate such a multitude. But according to those who wrote nostalgic memoirs of that

last grand Coppet summer, it would have been difficult
to find more brilliant talk in any other house in Europe.
"She has made Coppet as agreeable," Byron said about
Germaine and her domain, "as society and talent can
make any place on earth."[307]

A few days after Byron and her other guests left, five persons gathered into a room at Coppet to attend Germaine
de Staël's marriage to John Rocca. The only witnesses,
outside of the pastor, were the faithful Fanny Randall and
John's brother Charles, a judge. After officially announcing the birth of their son Louis Alphonse, and explaining
why they had heretofore been prevented from entering
into a formal marriage, Germaine and Rocca were pro-
nounced husband and wife. There was a curious clause in
the marriage contract, however, that had been inserted
at Germaine's insistence: "[The two parties...] for the
very plausible reasons by them enumerated...are obliged
to request that their marriage remain secret for a certain
amount of time."[308] The "plausible reasons" were fairly
obvious. It would have created a scandal if the existence
of "Little Us" had become officially known. And Germaine dreaded the loss of status she would suffer if the
marriage were made public. She had kept her promise to
Rocca, married him, and recognized their child. She was
not ready to do more. She would remain the Baroness de
Staël-Holstein, and the secret child would continue to live
in hiding at the home of Pastor Gleyre.

The will Germaine made shortly after her marriage
displayed her heartfelt religious inclinations and began

with a long eulogy to the love of her life—her father, Jacques Necker. "I commend my soul to God, Who has bestowed so many benefits to me chiefly through my father, to whom I owe what I am and what I have, and who would have spared me all my faults had I never turned away from his principles."[309] Among its final phrases: "I am secretly married to Monsieur Albert Jean de Rocca, as is proven by the marriage certificate joined to this testament. Our difference in age and political and private circumstances caused me to keep the marriage secret. . . . "[310] She left most of her money to her hidden son, and the remainder of her fortune to Rocca, Albertine, and Auguste, with additional gifts to Fanny Randall.

Having signed her will, she went back to Paris, looking forward to the birth of her daughter's first child. She arrived in October, in her own words "dead with fatigue" and "worn out by opium,"[311] and took up residence in the rue Royale. She again had political misgivings. The ultra-Royalists, though kept out of government so far by Louis XVIII, were greatly gaining in strength. In earlier years she would have instantly started a polemic against them, but now, out of sheer weariness, she was determined not to stir up any more trouble. "I might speak my mind frankly and say things that are not fashionable," she wrote Juliette; and, some months later: "I am determined to keep silent."[312] She felt more isolated than ever. Her relations with Montmorency, who would soon serve as Louis XVIII's foreign minister, were severely strained. But Barante, Guizot, and her son-in-law Broglie, who, strongly influenced by her political ideals, would play a pivotal role in overthrowing the Bourbon dynasty in 1830, came constantly to her salon. However ill and worn-out she felt, she was never more complaisant, more gracious, more amiable, than in those last months. Like the best of sovereigns and conversationalists, she had a gracious word for every member of her entourage: she questioned them frequently, listened intently to their answers, and led each of them to be more content with themselves. She grew to be more beloved than ever by these friends; and ironically, she would never be as influential as she was during the decade that followed her death.

Opium had strained her system to a greater degree than she could imagine. Her heart was weakening. Since her last stay in London she had been suffering from intense stomach pains—the opium-caused ailment that most tortured Coleridge. In February 1817, Germaine was walking up the stairs at a reception given by the Duc de Decazes, the king's foreign minister. Her son-in-law, Broglie, walking right behind her, saw her suddenly sway and fall. He caught her in his arms. Rocca, too sick to have gone out with his wife, rushed to her side when he heard her being carried into the house and put to bed. A cerebral stroke had felled her, her eyes were open but she could neither speak nor move. Her speech eventually returned, and her mind would remain lucid to the end. But her body remained paralyzed and she had to lie flat on her bed, plagued by cramps and bedsores. The Paris doctors who treated her misdiagnosed her as suffering from a liver ailment and prescribed unspeakable remedies, such as the consumption of crushed woodlice. By the time her Geneva physician reached her bedside, her case was hopeless.

Just before Albertine gave birth to her daughter, Germaine, unable to be with her, had sent her a small portrait of Necker, "in order that the new mother and child could feel his protection."[313] When Albertine's confinement ended, Germaine insisted that the usual schedules of festivities be resumed at her house, with Albertine doing the honors. One evening, Chateaubriand, after visiting Germaine, was asked to stay for dinner and found himself seated next to Juliette Récamier, whom he had not seen for ten years. United by their mourning for their mutual friend, they began a liaison that would last until the end of their lives and became legendary in French literary history.

After dinner, guests came to sit at Germaine's bedside. No possible physical suffering could have stopped her innate urge to communicate, to share ideas, to play with words. Chateaubriand was one of her most constant callers. "Good morning, my dear Francis!" she once addressed him in English. "I'm suffering, but that does not keep me from loving you."[314] It is to him that she noted, upon his last visit, "I have always been the same, lively and sad. I have loved God, my father, and liberty."[315] Another visitor was an American scholar, George Ticknor, of Boston, to whom she prophesied, about the United States: "You are the vanguard of the human race. You are the world's future."[316] Yet another friend had longed to see her: Constant had repeatedly asked to visit Germaine, but her family refused, fearing that the sight of him would upset her too much.

When spring came, Germaine was moved to another house that belonged to her son-in-law, one with a garden on the rue Neuve-des-Mathurins. Rocca, skeletally thin and barely able to stand, remained constantly at her side as she was driven through the garden in a wheelchair. The thought of dying in her sleep terrified her, and so she refused to sleep, or to take the opium that would ease her pain and bring her rest. Bonstetten relates the following detail concerning Rocca's extraordinary devotion to Germaine: "He begged her to sleep for at least five minutes, and swore that at the end of five minutes he would wake her. This he did. Then she slept for ten minutes. Rocca, watch in hand, waked her. Then twenty minutes. Thus, little by little, she became used to sleeping again."[317]

But by mid-July signs of gangrene began to appear on her body. The greatest doctors, Genevese as well as Parisians, agreed that her ailment, probably a cancer of the spinal bone marrow, was incurable. On her last day, sitting in her wheelchair, she received the Duc d'Orléans, the future King Louis-Philippe. That same evening she told Rocca, whose tuberculosis was getting worse, "This winter we shall go to Naples." They said good night to each other, and Fanny Randall stayed at Germaine's bedside. Germaine begged her for a draught of opium, which doctors had recommended she temporarily stop taking, to ease her pain. Fanny refused at first but finally gave in after Germaine's repeated pleas. She made it a rather strong dose, in hopes that it would last the patient a few hours. "Now are you going to sleep?" Fanny asked. "Heavily, like a big peasant woman,"[318] Germaine answered. Both women fell asleep, Fanny holding Germaine's hand.

For the past several weeks Auguste and the Duc de Broglie had been taking turns sleeping in the room next to Germaine's. The next morning Broglie rose at 5 a.m. to look in on his mother-in-law. He gently touched her hand and realized that it was ice-cold. It was July 14, 1817, the twenty-eighth anniversary of the Revolution Germaine de Staël had so cordially welcomed. She was only fifty-one years old.

Schlegel and Auguste escorted the hearse from Paris to Coppet, where Rocca, the Broglies, Ms. Randall, Bonstetten, and the rest of Germaine's intimates had preceded them. The day before the burial, in the sole presence of the Duc de Broglie, a group of workmen pierced the walled-up door to the Necker mausoleum. In the black marble basin, still filled with alcohol, lay Necker and his wife, half-covered with a large red cloak. One might surmise that Broglie did not make too great an effort to look, but he later reported that Necker's face was perfectly preserved, and that Madame Necker's head was hidden by the cloak.

On the following day, the coffin was carried from Germaine's house to the burial vault by four members of Coppet's municipal council, who wished to honor "the memory of the benefactress of the poor." All of the village's inhabitants had gathered at the burial site. It is said to have been a superb day, it is said that the outline of the Alps sparkled with unusual brightness against the azure sky. Bonstetten would also remember the unusually brilliant singing of the birds, the sound of leaves being crushed by the mourners' steps. The coffin was placed, as Germaine had wished, at the foot of the marble basin where her parents reposed, and then the vault was walled up again. Coppet's citizens will tell you that it has not been opened since.

Epilogue

A fortnight after Germaine's death, Benjamin Constant wrote Juliette Récamier: "I am sad but above all so indifferent. I uselessly exhort myself to take interest in something, but it does not work. Neither success nor failure mean anything to me...in sum I do not live anymore."[319] Yet whatever his grief for the loss of the woman who had been at the center of his life for a quarter of a century, it is only after her passing that Constant was able to fulfill himself: He shone as a deputy; he became one of France's most celebrated champions of liberalism; he was a popular idol in the Revolution of 1830. Would he have been honest enough to admit that he was utterly beholden to Germaine for his central role in the French liberal tradition?

"The trouble-maker," as Albertine called Constant, suffered from poor health in his last decade and had to walk on crutches. He died in late 1830, a few months afer the July Revolution and the coronation of Louis-Philippe, under whose reign he'd hoped to make another fortune. He received the honors of a national funeral— one fraught, in Constant tradition, by some tragicomic events. Early in the funeral procession, his hearse, which he had specified should be of unusually large size, collapsed under its own weight. A band of student acolytes carried his coffin upon their shoulders to Père Lachaise cemetery. Once the mourners had assembled at the grave, the aging Lafayette, just before delivering his funeral oration, lost his balance and nearly fell into the burial pit himself.

Mathieu de Montmorency was as overwhelmed as Constant by Germaine's passing. In the course of his brilliant career—he served as minister of foreign affairs, and held several important ambassadorial posts—he always found a few hours on July 14, the anniversary of Germaine's death, to commemorate her passing by writing recollections of her. Another man she had loved, Prosper de Barante, became famous upon the publication of his *Histoire des Ducs de Bourgogne* and other literary works, all the while enjoying a stellar diplomatic career that included an ambassadorship to St. Petersburg. Elected to the Académie Française, he became controversial for deploring the increasing materialism that plagued France under the reign of Louis-Philippe, a censure that Germaine most certainly would have joined him in expressing.

Jean Rocca died of tuberculosis six months after his wife. He spent much of his last months watching his frail son through a glass partition at Hyères, where he had taken him after Germaine's death, and imagined that his beloved "Little Us" was growing sturdier under his care.

It was only five days after Germaine's death, upon the reading of her will, that Albertine and her brother Auguste heard of the existence of "Little Us." Immediately after

Rocca's death, Auguste rushed to fetch the boy, who would be warmly taken into the Broglies' family and brought up alongside their own children. But although he did better than might be expected under the solicitous care of his siblings, Louis Alphonse remained a childish creature, filled with manias, terrified of imaginary threats and perils. This wan, timid young man, married, ironically, a granddaughter of Narbonne and died in 1838, at the age of twenty-six, leaving no issue.

Schlegel, whom Germaine had named to be her literary executor along with Auguste, would edit her *Considérations sur la Révolution francaise,* published the year after her death. Too conservative for radical youth, far too liberal for the "Ultras," *Considérations* became one of France's most widely-read and ardently disputed books, and led Staël to be looked on as the pioneer of revolutionary historiography. Its merciless account of Napoleon's rise and fall, and its plea for a British-style constitutional government, would turn *Considérations* into the Bible, for some decades, of French liberal thinkers. As for Schlegal himself, to whome Germaine had willed, in perpetuity, the use of his apartment at Coppet, he remained there for a few years, then returned to Germany, where he resumed his literary activities and made a second marriage that was no happier than the first one. He died in Bonn in 1845, having been awarded many academic honors.

In spite of her scandalous aura and a love life that shocked many of her contemporaries, Germaine had always managed to retain the deep affection and respect of her children. Auguste de Staël, who had inherited Coppet, married an English woman, had no heirs, and died young, at the age of thirty-three, having devoted most of his years to editing the works of his grandfather, Jacques Necker. His wife, who was to live until the 1870s, left Coppet to Albertine's daughter, Louise de Broglie, Comtesse d'Haussonville. The Haussonvilles' descendants own the estate to this day.

Having been endowed with the great beauty lacking in her mother, Albertine was also of a moral mettle different from Germaine's: she was very pious, with an extreme sense of propriety. But this bluestocking had a great heart, and she dedicated the rest of her brief life—she died in her forties—to the cult of her mother's memory. This filial love may have led Albertine to protect her mother's reputation with too excessive a zeal. Indulging in a tactic frequent among prudish offspring, she burnt a good part of her mother's correspondence. Into the fire went the majority of the letters written to Germaine by Benjamin Constant, a number of missives from Récamier, and all the ones written her by Ribbing and Narbonne. Fortunately Albertine could not put her hands on the letters her mother had written to those men, or to Souza, or to O'Donnell, or to Prosper de Barante. Albertine's goal was to have her mother's reputation exclusively grounded on her genius as a writer, obliterating the renown she acquired for her tempestuous *amours*. And her failure to puritanize her mother much enriches our knowledge of Germaine de Staël's complex and tormented inner life.

Benjamin Constant and his probable daughter Albertine, whom he much loved, maintained warm relations until they fell out over the issue of Constant's writings. Albertine had already disliked *Adolphe* and their relations were further chilled by his disapproval of the staunchly agnostic book on comparative religion that he published in the mid-1820s. The two separated bitterly and seldom saw each other again.

However different she was from her mother, Albertine had inherited some of Germaine's finest traits: great intelligence; immense generosity; a powerful sense of duty that, in the words of a contemporary, verged on "the austerity of stoicism." She was also endowed with a grace of manner and of conversation that enabled her to have Paris's most brilliant salon, as her grandmother's and her mother's had been. It was attended by Germaine' surviving friends and particularly by those of Albertine's husband, who went on to have a fine political career under Louis-Philippe: Victor de Broglie served as minister of foreign affairs, and then as ambassador to Great Britain. A prim, austere fellow but a dedicated liberal, he would be hailed after his death in 1870 as one of the most remarkable men of his generation, his powerful political vision having compensated for his less-than-winning manner.

Some of the Broglies' four offspring would have equally illustrious careers.

Their son Albert de Broglie, for instance, would serve as minister of public instruction, as president of the *Conseil d'État*, and, like his father, as ambassador to Great Britain. In later generations the Broglies continued to produce gifted politicians, great men of science. In sum, it is through the female line that Germaine's genius was perpetuated, a mode of descendance that might have greatly pleased her.

Such were some of the survivors who had been most affected by the loss of Germaine de Staël, who were fortunate enough to benefit from her prodigal largesse, her endless intellectual curiosity, her loyalty in friendship, her eccentric extravagance, and the fiery vitality that she so powerfully radiated to others and that made her so legendary. So legendary, in fact, that she would recur with increasing frequency in the writings of others. She was featured, for instance, in the works of the lavishly popular novelist Gyp (pen name for Sybille-Gabrielle de Mirabeau, Comtesse de Montel de Janville, 1849–1932), a prolific French novelist who published over 100 best-selling books and was admired by readers as diverse as Friedrich Nietzsche, Anatole France and Henry James. In Gyp's novel "Bijou," a group of young people in a large country house are planning to stage a play whose characters include Madame de Staël; they can't decide which member of the group is going to play her.

"Henri can very well play Mme de Staël," says one member of the group. "He has almost no mustaches."

"I?" says [Henri], taken aback, "I, play Mme de Staël?"

"She was rather masculine, you'll do very well."

"But for heaven's sake, I don't want to display myself to people who know me with a décolleté, a turban. . . . that would be hideous."

Decades after her death, those of her surviving friends who were questioned about Germaine de Staël would answer that anyone who had not known her, heard her, been engulfed by the power she emanated, could possibly have a notion of what she was like. The wisest of these friends would have emphasized that she was not only a uniquely dazzling personality but a dutiful, perpetually engaged (and enraged) political activist, and that she was above all a writer with a unique dedication to her craft. No comment would have more delighted her than the following, uttered shortly after her death by Prosper de Barante: "I would wish France to become more literary again. This would result in a wittier and more reasonable society."[320]

Notes

CHAPTER 1

1   Maria Fairweather, *Madame de Staël* (New York: Carroll & Graf Publishers, 2005), 33.

2   Comte de Montbrison, ed., *Memoirs of the Baroness d'Oberkirch* (London, 1852), 1:3.

3   Vicomte d'Haussonville, *Le Salon de Madame Necker* (Paris: 1882), 1:113–114.

4   Comte Fedor Golovkine, *Lettres diverses recueillies en Suisse, Genève et Paris* (1821), 292.

5   J. Christopher Herold, *Mistress to an Age: A Life of Madame de Staël* (New York: Grove Press, 2002), 23.

6   Benedetta Craveri, *The Age of Conversation* (New York: New York of Review Books, 2006), 369.

7   Ibid., 369–70.

8   Jean-François Marmontel, *Mémoires* (Paris: Mercure de France, 1999), 332.

9   Craveri, 368.

CHAPTER 2

10   Ghislain de Diesbach, *Madame de Staël* (Paris: Librairie académique Perrin, 1983), 37, citing Madame Rilliet-Hubert, "Notes sur la jeunesse de Madame de Staël," in *Occident*, March 1943.

11   Herold, 27.

12   Madame de Staël, *De l'Allemagne* (Paris: Flammarion, 1968), vol. 1, part 1, ch. XI: 101.

13   Madame de Staël, "Journal de jeunesse," June 29, 1785, in *Occident*, no. 3/4, 1932.

14   Herold, 43.

15   Staël, "Journal de jeunesse."

16   Herold, 37.

CHAPTER 3

17   Staël, "Journal de jeunesse," 240.

18   Madame de la Tour du Pin, *Memoirs of Madame de la Tour du Pin* (Toronto: Century Publishing, 1985), 97.

19   Diesbach, 68, citing A. Vivié, *Lettres de Gustave II à la*

comtesse de Boufflers, 368.

20   Lettres de l'impératrice
     Catherine II à Grimm,
     1774–96 (St. Petersburg: A.
     Grot, 1878).

21   Herold, 48.

22   Madame de Staël,
     Correspondance générale
     (Paris: Jean-Jacques
     Pauvert), vol. 1, part 1:58,
     letter to her mother, 29
     January 1786.

23   Herold, 62.

24   Ibid., 64.

25   Comte d'Haussonville, *Le
     Salon de Madame Necker*
     (Paris, 1882), vol. 2:184.

26   Craveri, 374.

27   Herold, 470.

28   Staël, *De l'Allemagne*, vol. 1,
     part 1, ch. XI: 101.

29   Herold, 74.

CHAPTER 4

30   Gouverneur Morris, *Diary
     and Letters*, ed. Anne Cary
     Morris (London: Kegan,
     Paul, Trench & Co., 1889),
     1:188.

31   Ibid., 278–79.

32   *Encyclopaedia Britannica*,
     15th ed., s.v. "Talleyrand."

33   Duff Cooper, *Talleyrand*
     (New York: Grove Press,
     2003), 28.

34   Herold, 94.

35   Ibid., 77.

36   Staël, *Correspondance
     générale*, vol. 1, part 2:239–
     40.

37   Madame de Staël,
     Considérations sur la

     Révolution française (Paris:
     Taillandier, 2000), 140.

38   Herold, 81.

39   Fairweather, 87.

40   Staël, *Considérations,* 157.

41   Herold, 84.

42   Staël, *Considérations,* 167.

43   Ibid., 168.

44   Staël, *Considérations,* 212.

45   Ibid., 213.

46   Herold, 98.

47   Ibid., 103.

48   Ibid.

49   Ibid.

50   Ibid., 106.

51   Ibid.

52   Ibid.

53   Alma Söderhjelm, *Fersen
     & Marie Antoinette* (Paris,
     1930), 227.

54   Herold, 112.

55   Staël, *Considérations,* 273.

56   Staël, *Correspondance
     générale*, vol. 2, part 2:354.

57   Staël, *Considérations,* 276.

CHAPTER 8

58   Staël, *Considérations,* 284.

59   Ibid., 285.

60   Ibid.

61   Herold, 121,

62   Fairweather, 153.

63   Herold, 123.

64   Madame d'Arblay, *Diary
     and Letters*, vol. 5, 1789–
     1793 (London: H. Colburn,
     1854), 339–42, letter of 22
     February, 1793.

65   Fairweather, 182.

66   Herold, 126–27.

67   Ibid. 124.

68   Ibid. 125.

69 D'Arblay, 348.

70 Georges Solovieff, ed., *Lettres de Madame de Staël à Narbonne* (Paris: 1960), 152.

71 Diesbach, 137.

72 Staël, "Réflexions sur le procés de la Reine," in *Oeuvres complètes de Mme la baronne de Staël* (Paris: Treuttel et Würtz, 1821), 1:1–33, also cited in Fairweather, 179.

73 Fairweather, 181.

74 Staël, *Correspondance générale*, vol. 2, part 1: 172–3.

75 Herold, 129.

76 Staël, *Correspondance générale*, vol. 1, part 2, 550–53, letter of 18 January 1794.

CHAPTER 9

77 *Lettres de Benjamin Constant à sa famille* (Paris, 1888), letter of 18 February 1788.

78 Herold, 151.

79 Ibid., 153.

80 Ibid.

81 Béatrice Jasinski, *L'Engagement de Benjamin Constant* (Paris: Minard, 1971), 13.

82 Herold, 154.

83 Tess Lewis, "Madame de Staël: The Inveterate Idealist," *Hudson Review*, vol. 54, no. 3 (Autumn 2001).

84 B. Jasinski, 10.

85 Fairweather, 201.

86 Herold, 155.

87 Letter from Talleyrand, 5 July 1797, quoted in Francine Du Plessix Gray, *At Home with the Marquis de Sade* (New York: Simon and Schuster, 1999), 349.

88 Herold, 167.

89 Ibid., 168.

90 Ibid., 173.

91 Ibid., 175.

92 Fairweather, 232.

93 Lady Blennerhassett, *Mme de Staël and Her Influence in Politics and Literature,* 3 vols. (London: Chapman and Hall, 1889), letter to Meister of 24 July 1797.

CHAPTER 10

94 Madame de Staël, *Dix années d'exil* (Fayard: Paris, 1996), 73.

95 Ibid., 51.

96 Herold, 343.

97 Simone Balayé, *Mme de Staël: Écrire, Lutter, Vivre* (Geneva: Librairie Droz, 1994), 138.

98 Staël, *Dix années d'exil*, 51.

99 Herold, 214.

100 Ibid.

101 Staël, *Dix années d'exil*, 56.

102 Ibid., 90.

103 Ibid., 54.

104 Ibid., 68.

105 Ibid., 74.

106 Paul Gautier, *Madame de Staël et Napoléon* (Paris: Plon, 1903), 8.

107 Staël, *Dix années d'exil*, 84.

108 Ibid., 99.

109 Herold, 182.
110 Staël, *Dix années d'exil*, 148.
111 Herold, 153.
112 Fairweather, 231.
113 *Mémoires et correspondance du roi Joseph par le Baron du Casse*, vol. 1, 1856–69 (Paris), 190, letter of 19 March 1801.
114 Staël, *Correspondance générale*, vol. 4, part 2:506, letter of 12 or 19 May 1802.

CHAPTER 11
115 Madame de Staël, *De la littérature* (Paris: Flammarion, 1991), 269–70.
116 Ibid., 267.
117 Ibid., 243.
118 Ibid., 245.
119 Ibid., 320.
120 Cited in *Dictionnaire critique de la Révolution française*, (Paris: Flammarion, 1992), 1054.
121 Ibid.
122 Ibid., 1055.
123 Ibid., 1058–59.
124 Staël, *De la littérature*, 335.
125 Ibid., 333.
126 Ibid.
127 Ibid., 415.
128 Ibid., 338.
129 Diesbach, 444.
130 Staël, *De la littérature*, 172.
131 Ibid., 87.
132 Madame de Staël, *De l'Allemagne*, vol. 2:301.
133 Ibid., 305.
134 Ibid., 302.
135 Ibid., 307.
136 Ibid., 303.
137 Ibid., 309.
138 Ibid., 306.
139 Staël, *De la littérature*, 401.
140 Ibid., 411.
141 Staël, *De l'Allemagne*, 125–26.
142 Staël, *De la littérature*, 416.
143 Ibid., 69.
144 Ibid., 406–7.
145 Gautier, 58.
146 Staël, *Dix années d'exil*, 88.
147 Herold, 222.
148 Ibid., 101.
149 Ibid., 151.
150 Ibid., 219.
151 Staël, *Dix années d'exil*, 86.
152 Ibid., 85.
153 Fairweather, 251.
154 Ibid.
155 Staël, *Correspondance générale*, vol. 4, part 1: 250, footnote 3.
156 Ibid., vol. 4, part 1:328–9, letter of 8 October 1800.
157 Benjamin Constant, *Journal intime* (Monaco: Editions du Rocher, 1945), 187, 190.
158 Fairweather, 270.
159 Herold, 275.
160 Ibid., 231.
161 Gautier, 103.
162 Herold, 247.
163 Alethea Hayter, *Opium and the Romantic Imagination* (Berkeley: University of California Press, 1968), 257.
164 Fairweather, 288.
165 Jean-Charles de Sismondi, *Fragments de son journal et correspondance* (Geneva, 1857), letter of 13 December 1830.

166 Herold, 245.
167 Ibid., 111.
168 Ibid., 247.
169 Ibid., 249.
170 Ibid.
171 Ibid., 250.
172 Ibid., 251.
173 Ibid.
174 Fairweather, 293.
175 Ibid.
176 Herold, 254.
177 Comte d'Haussonville, *Mme de Staël et Necker* (Paris: Calmann-Lévy, 1925), 335, letter from 28 October 1803.
178 Balayé, 53.
179 Ibid., 57.

CHAPTER 12
180 Herold, 259.
181 Ibid., 258.
182 Ibid., 259.
183 Ibid.
184 Staël, *Correspondance générale*, vol. 5, part 1:104, letter of 14 November 1803.
185 Herold, 261.
186 Ibid., 263.
187 Ibid., 264.
188 Ibid., 266.
189 Ibid., 103.
190 Constant, *Journal Intime,* 165.
191 Herold, 267.
192 Ibid., 268.
193 Ibid., 274.
194 Ibid., 276.
195 Staël, "Du caractère de Monsieur Necker et de sa vie," in *Oeuvres complètes,* 285.

196 Herold, 277.
197 Ibid., 280.
198 Ibid., 282.
199 Ibid., 296.
200 Maurice Levaillant, *The Passionate Exiles* (New York: Farrar Straus & Cudahy, 1957), 11.
201 Ibid.
202 Herold, 293.
203 Fairweather, 337.
204 Herold, 304.

CHAPTER 13
205 Herold, 307.
206 Ibid., 309.
207 Ibid., 310.
208 Ibid.
209 Ibid., 311.
210 Ibid., 312.
211 Diesbach, 374.
212 Herold, 342.
213 Fairweather, 337.
214 Herold, 327.
215 Ibid., 340.
216 Fairweather, 411.
217 Diesbach, 384.
218 Herold, 341.
219 Ellen Moers, *Literary Women* (New York: Doubleday and Co., 1976), 173.
220 Diesbach, 384.
221 Herold, 353.
222 Ibid., 356.
223 Ibid., 357.
224 Diesbach, 400.
225 Herold, 357.
226 Diesbach, 400.
227 Herold, 359.
228 Blennerhassett, 3:216.
229 Jean Mistler, *Madame de*

Staël et Maurice O'Donnell (Paris: Calmann-Lévy, 1926), 96.

230 Staël, *Correspondance générale*, 6:420–21, letter of 15 May 1808.
231 Herold, 375.
232 Fairweather, 338–39.
233 Herold, 380.
234 Ibid., 387.
235 Diesbach, 455.

CHAPTER 14
236 Herold, 401.
237 Staël, *Dix années d'exil*, 204.
238 Fairweather, 370.
239 Staël, *Dix années d'exil*, 206.
240 Ibid., 208.
241 Herold, 409.
242 Ibid., 410.
243 Ibid., 412.
244 Pierre Kohler, *Madame de Staël et la Suisse* (Lausanne: Payaut & Cie, 1916), 596.
245 Herold, 413.
246 Ibid.
247 Ibid., 414.
248 *Mémoires de la Comtesse de Boigne* (Paris: Mercure de France, 1999), 1:252.
249 Herold, 414.
250 Ibid., 415.
251 Ibid., 416.
252 Ibid., 417.
253 Ibid.
254 Ibid., 420.
255 Staël, *Dix années d'exil*, 262.
256 Ibid., 272.
257 Ibid., 269.
258 Ibid., 267.
259 Ibid., 294.
260 Ibid., 288.

261 Ibid., 268.
262 Ibid., 260.
263 Ibid., 289.
264 Ibid., 297.
265 Ibid., 272–73.
266 Ibid., 293.
267 Ibid., 300.
268 Ibid., 295.
269 Ibid., 304.
270 Ibid., 279.
271 Ibid.
272 Fairweather, 401.
273 Herold, 431.
274 Ibid.
275 Ibid.
276 Ibid., 436.
277 Fairweather, 414.
278 Ibid.
279 Herold, 444.
280 Ibid.
281 Ibid., 446.
282 Ibid., 447.
283 Blennerhassett, 3:504.
284 Herold, 440.
285 Ibid., 442.
286 Ibid., 444.
287 Diesbach, 509.
288 Herold, 446.
289 Ibid., 447.
290 Ibid.
291 Ibid., 448.

CHAPTER 15
292 Ibid., 450.
293 Fairweather, 442.
294 Herold, 452.
295 Staël, *Considérations*, 494.
296 Herold, 458.
297 Diesbach, 520.
298 Herold, 458.
299 Ibid.
300 Ibid., 461.

301 Ibid., 462.

302 Ibid.

303 Ibid., 464.

304 Lord Byron, *Byron's Letters and Journals*, vol. 4 (London: John Murray, 1924), 122, letter of 8 June 1814.

305 Herold, 465.

306 Byron, 5:109.

307 Herold, 466.

308 Herold, 466–67.

309 Fairweather, 466.

310 Herold, 467–68.

311 Ibid., 468.

312 Ibid.

313 Fairweather, 461.

314 Ibid., 462.

315 Ibid., 474.

316 Herold, 471.

317 Ibid., 470–71.

318 Ibid., 471.

EPILOGUE

319 Diesbach, 538.

320 Ibid., 548.

Bibliography

PRIMARY SOURCES

Madame de Staël. *Oeuvres complètes de Mme la baronne de Staël*. Publié par son fils. Paris: Treuttel et Würtz, 1821.

_____. *Considérations sur la Révolution francaise*. Présenté par Jacques Godechot. Paris: Tallandier, 2000.

_____. *Corinne, ou l'Italie*. [Place:] Gallimard, 1985.

_____. *Correspondance générale*. Texte établi et présenté par Béatrice Jasinski. Paris: Jean-Jacques Pauvert, [Year].

_____. *De l'Allemagne*. 2 vols. Paris: Flammarion, 1968.

_____. *De la littérature*. Paris: Flammarion, 1991.

_____. *Delphine*. 2 vols. Édition critique par Simone Balayé et Lucia Omacini. Genève: Librairie Droz, 1987.

_____. *Dix Années d'exil*. Édition critique par Simone Balayé et Mariella Vianello Bonifacio. Paris: Fayard, 1996.

BOOKS ON MADAME DE STAËL AND HER FAMILY

Balayé, Simone. *Madame de Staël*. Paris: Editions Klincksieck, 1979.

_____. *Madame de Staël: Écrire, Lutter, Vivre*. Genève: Librairie Droz, 1994.

Blennerhassett, Lady. *Mme de Staël and her Influence in Politics and Literature*, 3 vols. London: Chapman and Hall, 1889.

Diesbach, Ghislain de. *Madame de Staël*. Paris: Librairie académique Perrin, 1983.

Fairweather, Maria. *Madame de Staël*. New York: Carroll & Graf, 2005.

Gautier, Paul. *Madame de Staël et Napoléon*. Paris: Plon, 1903.

d'Haussonville, Comte. *Le Salon de Madame Necker*. 2 vols. Paris: Calmann-Lévy, 1882.

_____. *Mme de Staël et Necker*. Paris: Calmann-Lévy, 1925.

Herold, J. Christopher. *Mistress to an Age: A Life of Madame de Staël*. New York: Grove Press, 2002.

Kohler, Pierre. *Madame de Staël et la Suisse*. Lausanne and Paris: Payaut & Cie, 1916.

Mistler, Jean. *Madame de Staël et Maurice O'Donnell.* Paris: Calmann-Lévy, 1926.

Solovieff. *Lettres de Madame de Staël à Narbonne.* Préface de la Comtesse Jean de Pange, introduction notes et commentaires Georges Solovieff. Paris: Gallimard, 1960.

____. *Madame de Staël: Choix de texte, thématique et actualité.* Ezanville: Éditions Klincksieck, 1974.

GENERAL SOURCES

d'Arblay, Madame. *Diary and Letters.* Vol. 5, 1789–1854. [Place:] H. Colburn, 1854.

Boigne, Comtesse de. *Mémoires de la Comtesse de Boigne.* Paris: Mercure de France, 1999.

Byron, Lord. *Byron's Letters and Journals.* 12 vols. London: John Murray, 1924.

Casse, Baron du. *Mémoires et correspondance du roi Joseph.* Paris: [Publisher], 1856–69.

Catherine II of Russia. *Lettres de l'impératrice Catherine II à Grimm,* 1774–96. Saint Petersbourg: A. Grot, 1878.

Constant, Benjamin. *Adolphe.* Paris: Flammarion, 1989.

____. *Lettres de Benjamin Constant à sa famille.* Paris: [Publisher], 1888.

____ *Journal intime.* Monaco: Editions du Rocher, 1945.

Cooper, Duff. *Talleyrand.* New York: Grove Press, 2003.

Craveri, Benedetta. *The Age of Conversation.* New York: New York Review Books, 2006.

Furet, François, Mona Ozouf, and Bronislaw Baczko. *Dictionnaire critique de la Révolution française.* Paris: Flammarion, 1992.

Golovkine, Comte Fedor. *Lettres diverses recueillies en Suisse.* Genève and Paris: [Publisher], 1821.

du Plessix Gray, Francine. *At Home with the Marquis de Sade.* New York: [Publisher], 1999.

Hayter, Alethea. *Opium and the Romantic Imagination.* Berkeley and Los Angeles: University of California Press, 1968.

Jasinski, Béatrice. *L'Engagement de Benjamin Constant.* Paris: [Publisher], 1971.

Johnson, Paul. *Napoleon.* New York: Lipper/Viking Books, 2002.

Levaillant, Maurice. *The Passionate Exiles.* New York: Farrar Straus & Cudahy, 1957.

Marmontel, Jean-François. *Mémoires.* Paris: Mercure de France, 1999.

Morris, Gouverneur. *Diary and Letters.* Edited by Anne Cary Morris. London: Kegan, Paul, Trench & Co., 1889.

Oberkirch, Baronne d'. *Memoirs of the Baroness d'Oberkirch.* 3 vols. London: [Publisher], 1852.

Sismondi, Jean-Charles de. *Fragments de son journal et correspondance.*
    Geneva: [Publisher], 1857.
Söderhjelm, Alma. *Fersen & Marie Antoinette.* Paris: [Publisher], 1930.
Tour du Pin, Madame de la. *Memoirs of Madame de la Tour du Pin.*
    Toronto: Century Publishing, 1985.

PERIODICALS
Hudson Review 54, no. 3 (Autumn 2001).
Revue Occident (Paris, 1932).

Acknowledgements

My first and foremost debt is to James Atlas, my publisher, who with a wisdom which I hope is well-founded, decided that the irrepressible Germaine de Staël and I would make a perfect fit. His enthusiasm for this project, his constant readiness to listen compassionately to the occasional whining and fits of ill-humor that plague any writer confronted with a personality as complex as Staël's, has sustained me immeasurably.

Gratitude also to Alexander Rothman of Atlas & Co., whose diligent and patient nudging at every step of the writing process has enabled me to finish this book on schedule; to Marie d'Origny, who has served as research assistant for this biography with unfailing efficiency, exactitude and enthusiasm; to my friends Vincent Giroud, Claude Nabokov and Bernard Minoret, whose astute insights into French literature have been treasurable for more than one of my literary ventures; to George Lechner of the University of Hartford, who once more has guided me to numerous helpful texts; and to the omnivorous perspicacity and thoughtfulness with which my dear colleague Edmund White enhanced my book's ending by sharing a precious passage from a fin de siècle literary text.

To my beloved chum of a half century, Gabrielle Van Zuylen, enduring gratefulness for offering me a second home in Paris, my central base of operation for many of my literary undertakings, and for the support and inspiration she has offered me at every stage of my life. To my first readers—my eagle-eyed pals Jonathan Fasman, Joanna Rose and Jennifer Phillips, thank you from the bottom of my heart for offering me your innate and invaluable expertise as editors.

Finally, my thankfulness to the enormously kind staff of the Château de Coppet in Coppet, Switzerland—Germaine de Staël's family home—who graciously guided me through this lovely domain and offered me many new insights into my subject's quixotic character.